Building
Confidence
in Your
Child

Building Confidence in Your Child

Dr. James Dobson

© 1974, 1979, 1999 by James Dobson

Published by Revell
a division of Baker Publishing Group
P.O. Box 6287, Grand Rapids, MI 49516-6287
www.revellbooks.com

Spire edition published 2010
ISBN 978-0-8007-8811-7

Previously published under the title *The New Hide or Seek*

Printed in the United States of America

Scripture marked KJV is from the King James Version of the Bible.

Scripture marked TLB is taken from *The Living Bible*, copyright © 1971. Used by permission of Tyndale House Publishers, Inc., Wheaton, Illinois 60189. All rights reserved.

Scripture marked RSV is taken from the Revised Standard Version of the Bible, copyright 1952 [2nd edition, 1971] by the Division of Christian Education of the National Council of the Churches of Christ in the United States of America. Used by permission. All rights reserved.

Excerpts are used by permission from:
James Dobson, *Dare to Discipline* (Wheaton: Tyndale House, 1973).
Mike Michaelson, ed., *Growing Pains*, prepared cooperatively by the American Medical Association and the American Academy of Pediatrics.
Bill Gaither, lyricist, "Something Beautiful, Something Good," copyright © 1971 by Wm. J. Gaither.

10   11   12   13   14   15   16   7   6   5   4   3   2   1

This book is lovingly dedicated to children around the world who have reason to wonder if they are loved, respected, and valuable. It is our task as their parents and guardians to satisfy their inner longings, while also teaching them self-discipline, character, and respect for others. The words that follow are intended to assist adults in fulfilling that critical responsibility.

Contents

Preface to the Twenty-Fifth Anniversary Edition

Princess Diana was one of the most beautiful and glamorous women in the world. Paparazzi and fans followed her everywhere she went, and her likeness graced the covers of countless magazines. The "Diana look" influenced fashion and hairstyles in cultures around the world. When the princess died, millions mourned her tragic loss.

How could it be, given this international acclaim, that Diana suffered from a form of self-hatred? Is it conceivable that this most admired and emulated young woman suffered from a terrible body image, leading presumably to anorexia and bulimia? Those are very intriguing and disturbing questions that have implications for millions of us ordinary mortals.

The truth is that the values on which human worth depends in Western cultures are based on images of perfection marketed by the entertainment industry and the culture in general. They set an impossible standard of excellence for many individuals. Not even a beautiful princess could measure up to its imperious demands. Contestants in beauty contests, including the Miss America and Miss Universe pageants, are often aware of their flaws and shortcomings. If asked, they will divulge which aspects of their bodies they find frustrating and embarrassing. Some even seek surgical remedies for these perceived imperfections.

If the most beautiful and handsome people in the world often feel inadequate and insecure, what about today's teenagers? How is a gangly and immature kid supposed to deal with rejection and name-calling by those who are blessed with the coveted characteristics? And what about the individual who not only lacks a measure of physical attractiveness but also fails in school and faces other assaults on personal worth?

Indeed, it is this common scenario that led me in 1974 to address what I observed to be an "epidemic of inferiority" within a generation of children. At that time, I was an assistant professor of pediatrics at the University of Southern California Medical School and was working with many families who asked me how to help their kids cope with everyday pressures. Thus, I sat down to write a book eventually titled *Hide or Seek*, which offered ten strategies for parents and teachers seeking to build healthy and confident children. The book was an immediate bestseller and has continued as a classic of child rearing to this day.

As I write, twenty-five years have passed since *Hide or Seek* was first published. In that period, the popular culture has become even more vicious and unforgiving. Thus, it is very difficult to get our kids through adolescence without their experiencing some elements of self-hatred and loathing. Hollywood, the rock music industry, television, fashion models, and the internet make it clear to children and teenagers every day that some people are valuable and others are not. Those who don't measure up are "dissed" and treated like "geeks" and "nerds." In short, the need for advice on how to build confidence in children is greater than ever.

At times it seems that the pop culture is at war with families. For example, studies verify that 50 percent of nine-year-old girls and 80 percent of those ages ten to eleven have tried to diet because they perceive themselves to be fat. How sad that vulnerable kids feel compelled to be something they are not in order to avoid ridicule and rejection by their peers.

What is responsible for the destructive attitudes that continue to plague the young in cultures around the world? There are many logical answers, but I believe the American entertainment industry must take much of the blame. Its culpability is illustrated by a 1999 study conducted in the islands of the South Pacific after the penetration of Western television by satellite transmission. For the first time, teenagers began watching such programs as *Melrose Place* and *Beverly Hills 90210*. The attitudinal changes occurring have been dramatic, including the adoption of fashion and hairstyles of the television stars. More importantly, the girls began exhibiting symptoms of serious eating disorders.

Dr. Anne Becher, executive director of the Harvard Eating Disorder Center, studied sixty-five Fijian girls who watched television at least three times per week. She found that they were 50 percent more likely to perceive themselves as "too big" or "too fat" than other girls. Nearly two-thirds had attempted to lose weight in the past thirty days. What is even more distressing is that 15 percent of the girls said they had deliberately vomited to control their weight. In 1995, when television arrived, only 3 percent were bulimic. Clearly, the girls have been attempting more recently to emulate Heather Locklear and the other "skinny" but beautiful actresses. Fijian teenagers are learning what several generations of American girls have understood—that achieving "the look" is critical to social survival. This is why they do such foolish things as putting rings through the tips of their tongues, where millions of tiny nerves are located, or "decorate" their youthful bodies with tattoos that they will someday hate. Can there be any doubt that parents whose children are under this pressure and dozens of other cultural influences need help?

This is the background for my book, which is still relevant after all these years. However, the language was beginning to show the ravages of time. The illustrations had become dated, for example. Thus, we set about revising and updating the concepts that I had written when Richard Nixon was still the US President. The result is *Building Confidence in Your Child*, a copy of which you hold in your hand.

I introduced the original version with this explanation:

John McKay, the great football coach of the University of Southern California and the Tampa Bay Buccaneers, was being interviewed on television when the subject of his son's athletic talent was raised. That year John McKay Jr. was a successful player on his dad's college team. Coach McKay was asked to comment on the pride he must feel over his son's accomplishments on the field. His answer was most impressive: "Yes, I'm pleased that John had a good season last year. He does a fine job, and I *am* proud of him. But I would be just as proud if he had never played the game at all."

Coach McKay was saying, in effect, that John's football talent is recognized and appreciated, but his human worth does not depend on his ability to play football. Thus, his son would not lose respect if the next season brought failure and disappointment. John's place in his dad's heart was secure, independent of his performance. I wish every child could say the same.

To the contrary, human worth in our society is carefully reserved for those who meet certain rigid specifications. The beautiful people are born with it; those who are highly intelligent are likely to find approval; superstar athletes are usually respected. But no one is considered valuable just because he or she *is!* Social acceptability is awarded rather carefully, making certain to exclude those who are unqualified.

Believe it or not, a five-year-old is capable of "feeling" his or her own lack of worth in this system. Most of our little ones have observed very early that some people are valuable and some aren't; they also know when they are one of the losers! In many ways, we parents inadvertently teach this system to them, beginning in infancy to place a price tag on human worth. The result is widespread inferiority and inadequacy— which has probably included you and me in its toll.

There is a better way. This book is intended to help parents and teachers raise self-confident, healthy children. Our youngsters need not *hide* in shame; by applying the strategies I have outlined and others that parents can identify, we can give them the courage to *seek* the best from their world.

One background statement is needed before we continue. Controversy has arisen in the intervening years about what has been referred to as the "self-esteem movement." I agree with some of that criticism. Much of the behavior and many of the attitudes that have been taught in schools have an unpleasant aroma to them. For instance, I heard about an academic assignment recently that required high school students to write essays on "why I am so great." That is *not* what is needed by the younger generation.

This extreme approach to self-esteem has not been confined to the world of children; we've seen selfishness and arrogance run amok in this society, beginning three decades ago. Cultural analysts called the 1970s the "me generation." The 1980s became known as the "we generation," and "me-ism" was alive and well throughout the 1990s. Indeed, we are still "doing our own thing," "looking out for number one," "maximizing our potential," and "searching for self-fulfillment."

Self-absorption took a religious turn with the rise of the New Age philosophies, which elevated mankind to divine status. How better to vaunt your importance than to assert that you yourself are God or claim to know how to manipulate Him. The passage of time has confirmed that none of these self-serving slogans or teachings is healthy. Unchecked, the "me-first" attitude has the power to blow marriages apart, destroy businesses, and even subvert governments.

I lived for thirty-seven years in California where some sociologists believe selfishness in the modern era reached its apex. The old quip asked: "How many Californians does it take to screw in a lightbulb?" The answer: "Five; one to do the work and four to share the experience." But the fallout from the self-seeking philosophy is no laughing matter. Indeed, Scripture makes it clear that God hates arrogance, or what the inspired writers called "pride." There are 112 biblical passages that warn of this self-sufficiency, summarized by Proverbs 6:16–19. "These six things doth the LORD hate: yea, seven are an abomination unto him: A proud look, a lying tongue, and hands that shed innocent blood, An heart that deviseth wicked imaginations, feet that be swift in running to mischief, A false witness that speaketh lies, and he that soweth discord among brethren" (KJV).

Isn't it interesting that "a proud look" is listed first among God's seven most despised sins, apparently outranking adultery, profanity, and other acts of disobedience? Anything given that prominence in the Word must be considered carefully by those wishing to please the Lord. Before we can comply, however, we must interpret the meaning of the word *pride*. Language is dynamic, and the meaning of words changes with time. *Pride* has many connotations now that are different from the way that word was translated in the seventeenth century.

Today, a parent feels pride when a son or daughter succeeds in school or wins a race. I doubt that the Lord would be displeased by a father glowing with affection when he thinks of the boy or girl entrusted to his care. We speak also of the "Pride of the Yankees," or of a person who takes pride in his work, or of the pride of a Southern cook. These are positive attitudes that mean the individual is dedicated to his or her craft, or that he or she has self-confidence, or that the person will deliver what is promised. *Pride* in this usage is not the problem. Fortunately, most modern translations have updated the language to more faithfully link modern English to the ancient Hebrew text. The word commonly used in its place today is *haughtiness*. This casts an entirely different meaning on the warning.

What, then, is the biblical meaning of haughtiness? I believe it connotes an arrogance that leads us to violate the two most basic commandments of Jesus: to love God with all our heart, mind, and strength, and to love our neighbor as ourselves. A haughty person is too pompous to bow humbly before the Creator, confessing sins and submitting to a life of service to Him. Such arrogance produces hatefulness toward others, disregarding their feelings and needs. Most of the ills of the world, including war and crime, can be laid at the door of this sin. Perhaps this is why the writer of the proverb puts "a proud look" above all other evils. That is where it belongs.

I do not believe, by contrast, that the Bible condemns an attitude of quiet self-respect and dignity. Certainly those responses could not represent the pinnacle of the seven deadliest sins. Jesus commanded us to love our neighbors as ourselves, implying that we are permitted a reasonable expression of self-love. In fact, true love for others is impossible until we experience a measure of self-respect.

Some people actually believe that Christians should maintain an attitude of self-hatred in order to avoid the pitfall of haughtiness. After speaking to an audience in Boston, I was approached by an elderly woman who questioned my views. I had discussed the importance of self-confidence in children, and my comments contradicted her theology. She said, "God wants me to think of myself as being no better than a worm." She was referring, I suppose, to David's analogy in Psalm 22:6. "I would like to respect myself," she continued, "but God could not approve of that kind of pride, could He?"

I was touched by the words of this sincere woman. She told me she had been a missionary for forty years and had refused to marry in order to serve God more completely. While on a foreign field, she had become ill with an exotic disease that now reduced her frail body to ninety-five pounds. As she spoke, I could sense the great love of the heavenly Father for this faithful servant. She had literally given her life in His work, yet she did not even feel entitled to reflect on a job well done during her closing years on earth.

Unfortunately, this fragile missionary and thousands of other Christians were taught of their worthlessness. That teaching did not come from Scripture. Jesus did not leave His throne in heaven to die for the scum of the earth. His sacrifice was intended as the ultimate expression of love for that little woman and for all of His followers. He is not embarrassed to call us brothers and sisters. What a concept! If Jesus is now my brother, then that puts me in the family of God and guarantees that I will outlive the universe itself.

I certainly hope it is understood from this explanation that my book is not intended to promote *me-ism* in any form. Nor am I suggesting that selfishness be encouraged in children. That will occur easily enough without any help from parents. My purpose is to help mothers and fathers foster a quiet confidence that promotes inner physical, mental, and spiritual health.

But how about the practical side of the issue before us? How do you help a youngster who has trouble learning in school and thinks he is the dumbest member of the fourth grade? How do you comfort an eighteen-year-old who is the only one of her friends who has never had a boyfriend and sits at home alone during school functions? How do you help a child whose teeth protrude above his lower lip, or one who is blind, or deaf, or sick, or tiny, or too tall, or (fill in the blank). Don't tell me that parents of such children should ignore their pain, or that it is somehow unbiblical to even consider such things. Unfortunately, the popular obsession with self-esteem today has led some spiritual advisors to condemn those who have addressed these very real problems of childhood. I do not believe it. It is not unscriptural to care for those who are hurting, regardless of the age or the particular need. It is that obligation that led to the writing of the original *Hide or Seek*.

I pray that the strategies suggested in *Building Confidence in Your Child* will help parents protect their sons and daughters from the ravages of self-hatred. It *is* possible to raise healthy and confident children in a shock-wave world, if you put your mind and heart to it. May God bless you as you devote yourself to this important task.

Part 1

Values and Human Worth

1

The Epidemic of Inferiority

He began his life with all the classic handicaps and disadvantages. His mother was a powerfully built, dominating woman who found it difficult to love anyone. She had been married three times, and her second husband divorced her because she beat him up regularly. The father of the child I'm describing was her third husband; he died of a heart attack a few months before the child's birth. As a consequence, the mother had to work long hours from his earliest childhood.

She gave him no affection, no love, no discipline, and no training during those early years. She even forbade him to call her at work. Other children had little to do with him, so he was alone most of the time. He was absolutely rejected from his earliest childhood. He was ugly and poor and untrained and unlovable. When he was thirteen years old, a school psychologist commented that he probably didn't even know the meaning of the word *love*. During adolescence, the girls would have nothing to do with him, and he fought with the boys.

Despite a high IQ, he failed academically and finally dropped out during his third year of high school. He thought he might find acceptance in the Marine Corps; they reportedly built men, and he wanted to be one. But his problems went with him. The other marines laughed at him and ridiculed him. He fought back, resisted authority, and was court-martialed and thrown out of the Corps with a dishonorable discharge. So there he was—a young man in his early twenties—absolutely friendless and shipwrecked. He was scrawny and small in stature. He had an adolescent squeak in his voice. He was balding. He had no talent, no skill, no sense of worthiness. He didn't even have a driver's license.

Once again he thought he could run from his problems, so he went to live in a foreign country. But he was rejected there too. Nothing had changed. While there, he married a girl who herself had been an illegitimate child and brought her back to America with him. Soon, she began to develop the same contempt for him that everyone else displayed. She bore him two children, but he never enjoyed the status and respect that a father should have. His marriage continued to crumble. His wife demanded more and more things that he could not provide. Instead of being his ally against the bitter world, as he had hoped, she became his most vicious opponent. She could outfight him, and she learned to bully him. On one occasion, she locked him in the bathroom as punishment. Finally, she forced him to leave.

He tried to make it on his own, but he was terribly lonely. After days of solitude, he went home and literally begged her to take him back. He surrendered all pride. He crawled. He accepted humiliation. He came on her terms. Despite his meager salary, he brought her seventy-eight dollars as a gift, asking her to take it and spend it any way she wished. But she laughed at him. She belittled his feeble attempts to supply the family's needs. She ridiculed his failure. She made fun of his sexual impotence in front of a friend. At one point, he fell on his knees and wept bitterly, as the greater darkness of his private nightmare enveloped him.

Finally, in silence, he pleaded no more. No one wanted him. No one had ever wanted him. He was a most rejected man. His ego lay shattered in dust!

The next day he was a strangely different man. He arose, went to the garage, and took down a rifle he had hidden there. He carried it with him to his newly acquired job at a bookstorage building. And from a window on the sixth floor of that building, shortly after noon, November 22, 1963, he sent two shells crashing into the head of President John Fitzgerald Kennedy.

Lee Harvey Oswald, the rejected, unlovable failure, killed the man who, more than any other, embodied all the success, beauty, wealth, and family affection he himself lacked. In firing that rifle, he utilized the *one* skill he had learned in his entire, miserable lifetime.

Who Am I? Who Cares?

Oswald's personal problems do not excuse his violent behavior, and I would not absolve him of his responsibility. Yet an understanding of his inner torment and confusion helps us see him, not only as a vicious assassin but also as the pitiful, broken man. Every day of his life, from the lonely days of childhood to the televised moment of his spectacular death, Oswald experienced the crushing awareness of his own inferiority. Finally, as it often does, his grief turned to anger.

The greater tragedy is that Lee Harvey Oswald's plight is not unusual in America today. While others may respond less aggressively, this same consuming awareness of inadequacy can be seen in every avenue of life—in every neighborhood, in every church, and on the campuses of America's schools. It is particularly true of today's adolescents. I have observed that the vast majority of those between twelve and twenty years of age are disappointed with who they are and what they represent. In a world that worships superstars, they look in the mirror for signs of greatness and see only a terminal case of acne. Most of these discouraged young people will not admit how they feel because it hurts to acknowledge these inner thoughts. On our *Focus on the Family* radio program, several audience members have revealed deep-seated memories of inferiority:

Woman: In grammar school, I was made to feel very uncomfortable by the fact that I was intelligent. By the time I graduated, I had really determined that being smart was a very big disadvantage because I was set apart from everyone else.

Man: During the Depression years, a friend of ours brought some clothes over to our house because we had nothing to wear. My dad was so irate because they brought these things over, he made me gather them all up and take them back to his house. I felt very bad about it and very insecure because he felt he had to take these things away from me.

Woman: I was always the tallest in my class. In fifth grade they used to measure us once a month—and I was even taller than all the boys. When it came to dance, I had no one to dance with because they were all at my chin level.

Woman: I had the opposite problem. I was always the smallest, and I looked so young. I can remember my freshman year in college. I went home and went to the fair. We went up to a booth where they would guess your age—and he guessed me as 14. Everyone thought that was so hilarious.[1]

These inferiority feelings are quite common among children and adolescents. Almost everyone can remember some similar crisis of confidence.

As early as age three or four, we begin to ask basic self-worth questions: Who am I? Who needs me? Who cares about me? Will I be accepted? Will people laugh at me? Will I be able to compete with others? Do I have a place in this world? Does anybody love me? And every child begins gathering evidence to answer these questions. Each failure, each mistake, each time he speaks out of turn, each time she is not invited to a party or picked for a team, each time he is called a name—this all gets stored in the memory bank. When the child steamrolls into adolescence, all of this comes back with a volcanic force to attack his or her sense of self-worth.

I remember reading about a farmer who found a beautiful eagle down by the lake on his property. One of its legs had been caught in a steel trap. Despite that weight and its pain, the bird had flown many miles, but now it was exhausted. Low

25

self-esteem is like that. You can fly with it for a while, but it weighs you down. And unless you, or someone else, can find a way to deal with it—to remove that trap—it will ground you and possibly lead to your destruction. Sadly, the high incidence of teen suicide may relate largely to a lack of confidence.

The vast majority of those between twelve and twenty years of age are disappointed with who they are and what they represent.

Oswald never published his early self-doubts and loneliness—nor would we have paid much attention if he had. But in retrospect there is little doubt that the overwhelming rejection of his early childhood led to deep discontent as a teenager, to his twisted adult life, and to his dark destiny. Not everyone who suffers through a bad childhood becomes an assassin, although it is sobering to consider the published case studies of Gary Gilmore, David Berkowitz, and Ted Bundy. Yet the consequences of low self-esteem can be grim for others as well. We need to start early in preparing our children for the many onslaughts they will face.

You see, every stage of life poses its own unique threats to confidence. As I mentioned, little children face substantial fears about their status and identity, and teenagers must deal with a whirlwind of threatening change. Many adults also struggle with the legacy of inferiority feelings. I am also convinced that senility and mental deterioration at the latter end of life often result from the growing awareness by the aged that they live in the exclusive world of the young. Their wrinkles, backaches, and dentures are scorned. Their ideas are out-of-date. Their continued existence is a burden. This feeling of uselessness is the special reward that we reserve for life's survivors, and it should not be surprising that the elderly often "disconnect" intellectually.

Thus, if inadequacy and inferiority are so universally prevalent at all ages of life, we must ask ourselves "Why?" Why can't our children grow up accepting themselves as they are? Why do so many feel unloved and unlovable? Why are our homes and schools more likely to produce despair and self-hatred than quiet confidence and respect? Why should each child have to bump his head on the same old rock? These questions are of major significance to every parent who would shield his child from the pain of self-hatred.

False Values, True Worth

The current epidemic of self-doubt has resulted from a totally unjust and unnecessary system of evaluating human worth. This system is prevalent in our society. Not everyone is deemed worthy; not everyone is accepted. Instead, we reserve our praise and admiration for a select few who have been blessed from birth with the characteristics we value most highly. It is a vicious system, and we, as parents, must counterbalance its impact. This book is dedicated to the proposition that all children are created worthy and must be given the right to personal respect and dignity. It can be done!

In order to help parents understand what their children are facing, part 1 will analyze the false values on which self-esteem so often depends in our culture. I hope the reader will see how effectively, and often unknowingly, we teach our small children that worthiness and social approval are beyond their reach. By glorifying idealized models, to which few can conform, we have created a vast army of "have-nots"—born losers who are discouraged with life before it has really begun. Like Lee Harvey Oswald, they turn this way and that, searching vainly for a solution to the inner emptiness and pain. For the millions who never find it, the road to personal worth becomes a long, unpaved detour leading nowhere.

The matter of personal worth is not only the concern of those who lack it. In a real sense, the health of an entire society depends on the ease with which its individual members can gain personal acceptance. Thus, whenever the keys to self-worth are seemingly out of reach for a large percentage of the people, as in Western society at the turn of the twenty-first century, then widespread "mental illness," neuroticism, hatred, alcoholism, drug abuse, violence, and social disorder will certainly occur. Personal worth is not something human beings are free to take or leave. We must have it, and when it is unattainable, everybody suffers. Of course, the root cause of all human suffering is sin in individuals and in the human family. It is often expressed in social forces that devalue human worth and make life miserable for the most vulnerable among us.

Personal worth is not something human beings are free to take or leave. We must have it, and when it is unattainable, everybody suffers.

But I have not written this book merely to discuss our problems or even to criticize the society that creates them. Rather, I propose a better way: By a proper use of parental influence and direction, we can provide our children with the inner strength necessary to survive the obstacles they will face. We can open the road to self-esteem and personal worth. Perhaps we won't reconstruct the world, but we can certainly help our children cope with it more successfully.

The heart of this book, part 2, is devoted to a description of ten comprehensive "strategies" for building self-esteem, each one focusing on a particular area of concern. These discussions offer specific answers and recommendations regarding the common threats to personal worth surrounding our children. Some of the topics included are:

Strategies for the Early Years

- Building an esteemed-child environment at home
- Conveying respect as well as love
- Combating routine panic and parental fatigue
- Confronting sibling rivalry and a child's feeling that parental love must be won
- Dealing with the false ideals modern life puts before young eyes
- Instilling positive self-attitudes early

Strategies for Middle Childhood

- Helping your child compensate for weaknesses by working on strengths
- Preparing your child to compete in a competitive world
- Shaping the will without breaking the spirit
- Reducing educational threats to esteem
- Instilling independence and responsibility
- Teaching a child to be sensitive to others

Strategies for Adolescence

- Preparing a child for adolescence
- Meeting adolescent feelings of rejection
- Building healthy sexual attitudes
- Easing the process of breaking away

Strategies for Adulthood

- Identifying sources of depression
- Confronting deep-seated feelings of inferiority
- Therapeutic giving to others

Following the discussion of these strategies, part 3, chapter 9, is a concise explanation of patterns of human behavior. It describes the strategies or patterns used by both children and adults in fighting the values wars. This chapter is recommended to one who wants to comprehend the meaning behind the behavior of a child or spouse, a neighbor, or even of oneself. It is followed in chapter 10 by some final comments and observations about the source for true values and human worth.

Before we can resolve the problems confronting our children, however, we must understand the predicament they face. Let's move back, then, into the world of the young, examining the destructive value system taught so effectively throughout the formative years of life. Parents and teachers can contribute greatly to the self-respect of the next generation if they can genuinely empathize with little people—seeing what they see, hearing what they hear, and feeling what they feel.

2

Beauty

The Gold Coin of Human Worth

Former late-night television personality Johnny Carson once described the delicate situation when a new mother shows you an unattractive baby. What do you say, as she proudly holds out her little bundle? Carson concluded that the only safe remark is, "My, that sure is a baby, isn't it?" He was right that a mom is never so vulnerable as in that moment, and the onlooker had better choose words *very* carefully. Why? Because in our society, a beautiful baby is a more valuable human being than an unattractive one.

Without question, the most highly valued personal attribute in many cultures is physical attractiveness. Accordingly, the personal worth of a newborn infant is anxiously evaluated by parents as they examine the little body and its accessories. The parents had secretly hoped to give birth to a grinning, winking, blinking, six-week-old Gerber baby, with four front teeth and rosy, pink cheeks. Instead, medical personnel handed them a red, toothless, bald, prune-faced, screaming little creature they may occasionally feel like sending back. You see, the personal worth of that one-day-old infant is actually doubted by the parents. Soon afterward, however, the parents learn to appreciate that face that only a parent could love—but other people don't. And this point must be emphasized: *We adults respond very differently to an unusually beautiful child than to a particularly unattractive one, and that difference has a profound impact on a developing personality.* The pretty child is much more likely to see the world as warm and accepting. The ugly child is far better acquainted with the cold, steely eyes of rejection.

Beauty and the Baby

When my daughter was fifteen months of age, her physical features seemingly appealed to adults. Her mother dressed her attractively. Considerable warmth and affection were shown to Danae wherever she went. People would hold her in their arms, tease her, and give her candy. The attention she received is typically given to any child who is thought to be cute or attractive. It is neither sought nor earned; it is given spontaneously by the adult world. However, three months after her first birthday, Danae rearranged her features for the worse.

I had driven home from the hospital at the end of a workday and was met by my wife in the driveway. She was holding our little girl in her arms, and they were both splattered with blood. My wife quickly told me the painful details: Danae was learning to run, and her mother was playfully chasing her through the house. Suddenly the little toddler darted to the left, losing her balance. She fell into the sharp edge of a table in the living room, catching her front tooth squarely as she went down. The tooth had been driven completely into her gums, appearing to be knocked out. The inside of her lip was slashed, and she looked terrible.

My daughter's permanent tooth was not due for six years, but it could also have been damaged. Fortunately, however, that baby tooth refused to die. It gradually returned to its proper place, and the wound healed with no long-term damage. In fact, that same incisor made three more unscheduled trips into the gums before giving up the ghost four years later. It demonstrated uncanny courage in hanging on, despite the whacks and bumps it absorbed. By the time it finally turned loose, Danae considered her toothlessness to be a valuable status symbol in the neighborhood. At the time of the first accident, however, the situation appeared very discouraging.

Danae's head-on collision with the table temporarily distorted the shape of her mouth. Since the cut was on the inner part of her lip, she appeared to have been born that way. All the babyish appeal was now gone. The next evening I took her with me to a store, where I noticed that people were responding differently to her. They would look at her and then turn away. Instead of the warmth, love, and tenderness previously offered to her, rejection and coolness were unconsciously demonstrated. People were not trying to be mean; they simply did not find her attractive any longer. I was irritated by the reaction because it revealed the injustice in our value system.

How unfair, it seemed, to reward a child for something that had not been earned or to destroy another child for circumstances beyond control. Yet a child who is attractively arranged usually profits from the moment of birth on.

Justified complaints have been raised about beauty contests that offer scholarships and prizes to gorgeous babies, but they are still common—as if the attractive child doesn't already have enough advantages. Some of the worst excesses of this emphasis on beauty among the young came to widespread public exposure through coverage of the murder of JonBenet Ramsey. At an age when most little girls are making the transition from preschool to first grade, this youngster's life was a whirl of pageants and modeling in very adult, sophisticated makeup and clothing. Multitudes of children similarly are being pushed from toddlerhood headlong into this distorted system of evaluating human worth.

Beauty and the Child

Very early in life, a child begins to learn the social importance of physical beauty. The values of society cannot be kept from little ears, and many adults do not even try to conceal their bias. It is an oblivious child who fails to notice that the ugly do not become "Miss America," nor do they become cheerleaders. The ugly seldom star in movies, may not get married, and have fewer friends. The ugly are less desirable!

It is surprising just how effectively we teach our small children to appreciate the beauty cult. In examining the traditional literature of childhood, I was amazed to see how many stories, some centuries old, center around physical attractiveness. Consider:

- *The Ugly Duckling*. In this familiar story an unhappy little bird was rejected by the better-looking ducks. Symbolizing the plight of every unattractive child, the ugly duckling was disturbed by his grotesque appearance. Fortunately, a beautiful swan was inside and surfaced in young adulthood. The story does not mention any ugly ducklings who grew up to be ugly ducks! How many children wait patiently for their beautiful swan to appear but see things go from bad to worse during adolescence?

- *Sleeping Beauty*. Why was this story not titled "Sleeping Ugly"? Because the prince would not have awakened her with a gentle kiss. He would have let a homely little princess go on resting. Her beauty was an essential ingredient in the romantic tale.

- *Edward Scissorhands* and *The Man without a Face* are among movies that have made a particular point of attractiveness. Then, of course, there are the cartoon remakes of old classics *Beauty and the Beast* and *The Hunchback of Notre Dame*. The spirited Belle might have found the handsome prince rather a bore after getting to know the more interesting beast side of his character. But of course lovely Belle could never live happily ever after with an ugly mate.

- On stage, would we find the music of Andrew Lloyd Webber so poignant if "The Phantom of the Opera" wasn't so hideous looking? No way he could get the girl in the end either.

- *Rudolph, the Red-Nosed Reindeer*. Rudolph had a weird nose, which caused him to be rejected by his fellow reindeer. They laughed and called him names. They wouldn't let poor Rudolph join in any reindeer games. This story has nothing to do with reindeer; it has *everything* to do with children. This is how they treat the physically peculiar. The person who is different is rejected and ridiculed. The only way the world's "Rudolphs" can gain acceptance is to perform some miraculous feat, symbolized by the gallant sleigh ride through the fog.

- *Dumbo, the Elephant.* Dumbo was ridiculed for having big, floppy ears, until he used them to fly. The theme is remarkably similar to the plight of poor Rudolph. It appears repeatedly in the literature of the young because of its common occurrence in the lives of children themselves.

- *Snow White and the Seven Dwarfs.* The evil queen asked the fateful question, "Mirror, mirror on the wall, who's the fairest of them all?" I am still awed by the stupidity of her question, considering all of the possibilities to which a magic mirror might respond! Yet the motivation behind her request is clear: The fairest of them all was the most noble, worthy person in the land. Perhaps she still reigns.

- *Cinderella.* The primary difference between Cinderella and her two wicked stepsisters was a matter of beauty. Any illustrated edition of *Cinderella* reveals that fact. Sure, Cinderella was ragged and uncombed, but the basic ingredient was there. It wasn't the pumpkin and the mice that shook up the prince when Cinderella arrived at the ball. You can bet she was a pretty little thing.

This theme emphasizing beauty appears in more than fairy stories from long ago—current literature reflects it as well. The approved fourth-grade reader adopted as a California state textbook at one time carried a fairy story about three little girls. Two of the girls were very attractive, with beautiful hair and facial features. Because of their beauty they were loved by the people and given kingdoms to rule. The third little girl was very ugly. No one liked her because she was not pleasant to look at. The people would not let her have a kingdom of her own. She was unhappy and sad. The story ended on a bright note, however. This little girl was given a kingdom with the animals. Isn't that jolly? Her ugliness got her banished from the world of human beings, as it often does. Her physical deficiencies were described in considerable detail, so that similar children in the classroom would be stared and pointed at.

It is an oblivious child who fails to notice that the ugly do not become "Miss America," nor do they become cheerleaders.

Why must we emphasize this unattainable attribute so vigorously at every level of our society? The message comes through loudly and clearly: Really worthy folks are beautiful people. We have been treated to the classic pageant of that message, and its bitter consequences, in the British royal family. Prince Charles could have hardly found a more unsuitable personality match than Diana Spencer, but all the United Kingdom, and even the world, thrilled at this young, seemingly accomplished beauty. Only after the divorce and Diana's tragic death did the dark side of the fairy tale emerge, including Diana's extreme feelings of inferiority, her eating disorder, and her deep, unfulfilled need for affection and approval.

Most children are able to determine the relative worth of their own physical arrangement by the time they enter kindergarten. A thirty-six-year-old man told me, "I was five years old when I realized I was ugly, and I've never been the same since." His entire adult personality had been shaped (distorted) by that awful realization.

Another man, at age sixty, described his reaction to the beauty cult in such graphic terms that I wrote down his exact comment. He said, "I saw this clearly when I was twelve years old. I saw the injustice of it. I saw that it was nobody's fault, particularly, so I didn't get bitter about it. But I resigned myself to play the game of life with a short hand."

If a child is odd or noticeably different, he or she has certainly heard about that "deformity" from friends and neighbors during preschool days. Children can be terribly brutal to one another. Some youngsters feel it their personal mission in life to point out everyone else's flaws and deficiencies. The unusual or different boy or girl has been informed of his unique characteristics from his earliest recollection. Life can be very uncomfortable, indeed, for the child who is too fat or too thin, whose white skin is too ruddy or whose black skin is too light or dark, who is too tall or too short, or who is besieged by a tornado of freckles. A host of genetic and racial characteristics warrant derision. Disadvantaged is one whose nose curves up or down or to one side, whose hair is too curly or too straight, or who has big feet or a crossed eye, or protruding ears, or a large "behind." There are any number of distortions. The child's emotional reaction operates according to the weakest link in the chain. If there is a single embarrassing feature, the child will worry about that deficiency as though it were the most important thing in life.

This vicious aspect of childhood is often forgotten by busy adults. Transport yourself back for a moment into the world of the very young, where unconcealed aggression lies just below the surface. There you may have to fight to defend your honor, even if it costs you your front teeth. Name-calling, ridicule, and rejection are hurled at the weak like poisoned darts. Self-esteem teeters on the brink of disintegration with each perceived failure or mistake. This threatening aspect of childhood must be remembered if we hope to understand the next generation. Why, for example, would some children rather take forty lashes than go to a new school or perform in front of their peers? They know, but cannot explain, the pain that other children can inflict on their unprotected egos.

The note reproduced below was given to me by the mother of a fourth-grade girl, who found it on her desk. It was apparently written without provocation and illustrates the brutality with which one child can assault the self-esteem of another:

Awful Janet
Your the stinkest girl in this world. I hope you die but of course I suppose that's impossible. I've got some ideas.
1. Play in the road
2. Cut your throad
3. Drink poison
4. get drunk
5. knife yourself
Please do some of this you big fat Girl. we all hate you. I'm praying Oh please lord let Janet die. Were in need of fresh air.

Did you hear me lord cause if you didn't will all die with her here. See Janet we're not all bad.

From Wanda Jackson

What is "Awful Janet" to think about a venomous note of this nature? She may have the self-confidence to take it in stride, particularly if Wanda is a social failure herself. However, if Wanda is popular and Janet is not, the stage is set for a painful and enduring emotional experience. Notice that Wanda made reference to Janet's physical appearance ("you big fat Girl"), and she implied that a vast army of friends agreed with her ("we all hate you"). Those two ingredients would crush a sensitive child.

It has always been surprising to me to witness the emotional power of such an episode. If Janet was stung by the note, it will probably be remembered all through her life. Ask any adult to relate a similar incident from childhood, and you'll get an immediate response, describing an experience that may have occurred forty years ago. When I was in the sixth grade, for example, a classmate called me "skinny." He said it only once, yet I remember the event perfectly today. I would still like to blacken his eye. Why? Because my personal worth was questioned! Likewise, a middle-aged man told me he had been self-conscious about his excessive height when he was in junior high school. His mother was asked how she could find him in a crowd, and she replied, "I just look for the kid who's sticking up above everyone else." Zap! The arrow stuck in his heart, and he remembers it three decades later. He has forgotten every other happening of that month, but he can still hear his mother's words ring in his head. Comedian George Carlin always hated his name because his friends would sing:

Georgieporgie Puddininpie,
Kissed the girls and made them cry;
When the boys came out to play,
Georgieporgie ran away.

George said he was painfully aware of the vague references to his manhood in this goading chant.

Youngsters are highly skilled at composing nicknames to replace the titles carefully selected by another child's parents. These names are seldom intentionally vicious, but their impact is often devastating. They are usually derived from the victim's primary physical flaw, spotlighting and emphasizing the feature the person would most like to hide. Thus the boy with protruding teeth becomes "Bucky Beaver," the plump fellow is "Porker," the hairy girl is "Shag," the skinny boy is "Bones," the skinny girl is "Birdlegs," the large-framed young lady is "Moose," the tiny boy is "Runt" or "Pee Wee" or "Peanut." Lee Harvey Oswald was called "Ozzie Rabbit" in the Marine Corps. Josef Stalin was called "nine-toed one" because two of his toes were fused together. Examples of this kind of disrespect are innumerable.

I knew a small boy in junior high school who had a round head, thick glasses (which caused his eyes to appear bulged), and a very large mouth. The other students called him "Frog." It was a perfect nickname, except that Frog himself wasn't so proud of the analogy. It never occurred to his classmates that he might not want to look like a little green creature on a lily pad. The ultimate insult came when they asked Frog if he could cause warts on their hands and catch flies with his tongue. The child begins to identify with the nickname and suffers accordingly. How can Frog or Bucky or Moose or Bones regard themselves with respect when their friends see them as deformed and ridiculous? If you asked them to write an honest appraisal of "Who I am," they would begin by describing the one feature that causes the greatest personal dissatisfaction.

One educator suggests that teachers squelch name-calling in the classroom by asking such questions as "Why did you call him that?" or "How does the other person feel?" One child answered, "Calling someone a name is like throwing a brick at that person. They both hurt."

The educator adds, "Names *do* hurt, and children need to understand this. Name-calling is a purposeful attempt to diminish somebody's worth."[1]

Children are keenly aware of their relative worth among their classmates. Who, for example, is elected captain of the baseball team? Who is never even nominated? Who is chosen first in games and contests? Who is selected last? Who is invited to the important birthday parties? Who is excluded? How many Valentine's Day cards does an unpopular child receive, compared to the superstars? In her first-person article, "When You're Born a 2.5 Instead of a 10," Amy Russell describes the agony of high school dodgeball games "with the boys": "The pretty girls were highly prized and thus knocked off right away, leaving me and a few other losers quivering with mortification by the bleachers, praying for a quick out. Inevitably some guy would start the chant, 'Let's get Pelican Legs! Hey, Pelican Legs!'"[2] There are many simple and direct ways to evaluate one's social worth, and some children draw the same conclusion from each assessment: "I am a complete washout and a failure."

Teachers and psychologists have a more sophisticated technique for sampling social status among children. It is called a "sociogram." Each child in a classroom is asked to list the three children with whom he or she would like to be placed. Without informing the class of the results, the teacher can then tally the choices and identify the "stars" and the "isolates." A good teacher will then throw her support behind the rejected youngster. Unfortunately, however, teachers are products of the same society that molds the values and attitudes of everyone else. They are often repelled by the physically unattractive child and drawn to the "cutie." Certainly, every good teacher fights this inclination, some more successfully than others.

When shown a set of children's pictures and asked to identify the one who probably misbehaved, adults most often choose the least attractive child.

Researchers have discovered some alarming pro-beauty biases toward children:

- Evidence seems to indicate that attractive children get better grades.
- Adults expect unattractive kids to be troublemakers. When shown a set of children's pictures and asked to identify the one who probably misbehaved, adults most often choose the least attractive child. Ugly children were also considered more dishonest than their cuter peers. "For all the talk about character and inner values," write researchers Ellen Berscheid and Elaine Walster, "we assume the best about pretty people. And from grade school on, there's almost no dispute about who's beautiful."

- In disciplining children, adults tend to be easier on cuter kids. Even for the *same* misbehavior, the ugly child is punished more severely.[3]

It is no wonder, then, that children show this same bias, yet it occurs even at very young ages. In one study, two screens were suspended above babies' cribs. One screen showed the image of an attractive adult, the other screen the image of an unattractive adult. The babies tended to show a "significant preference" for the attractive image.[4]

Other research has found that cute nursery-schoolers are already enjoying greater popularity among their peers, while fat three-year-olds are already being snubbed.[5]

Deborah A. Byrnes, assistant professor of elementary education at Utah State University, summarizes the data like this:

Children and adults alike perceive physically attractive children as possessing more positive characteristics than physically unattractive children. Attractive children are considered more intelligent, successful, adjusted, and socially competent, and are expected to do well and be good. Unattractive children are more likely to be seen as dishonest, unpleasant, chronically antisocial, and having low self-concepts. As a result of these stereotypes: attractive children tend to have enhanced social opportunities, whereas unattractive children have limited ones. . . . Attractive children receive more help, smiles, prosocial verbal comments, and physical affection. . . . Attractiveness stereotypes appear to be more stringently applied to females than males. . . . Even teachers often perceive attractive children to be more intelligent, more interested in school, and more likely to succeed academically and socially than unattractive children. . . .

The significance of attractiveness in society would be difficult for children to ignore. Its importance is modeled for them daily. At a young age, children begin equating beautiful people with goodness, pleasure, and status; ugly people are seen as bad, frightening, and inferior. Given this, we should not be surprised that children tend to seek out attractive children as friends and avoid unattractive children.[6]

What a distorted system of values we propagate! What irreparable damage is done to an unattractive child whose parents do not intervene as allies. Every day he or she is confronted by awful inferiority. He can neither explain nor apologize. She can't even hide. Cruel voices follow her wherever she goes, whispering their evil messages in her childish ears: "The other children don't like you." "See, I told you you'd fail." "You're different." "You're foolish." "They hate you." "You're a failure." "You're worthless!" As time passes, the voices get louder and louder, until their scream obliterates all other sounds in an adolescent's mind: "There's no hope; you are doomed!"

Beauty and the Adolescent

If physical attractiveness is considered important during childhood, it becomes supersignificant and allconsuming during adolescence. For a period of four to six years following puberty, the child's entire physical and emotional apparatus is focused on the exciting new world of sex. Both boys and girls think about it, dream about it, fantasize about it, and too often set out to do something about it. Adolescents are aflame with sexual curiosity, romanticism, and sheer biological passion. Now obviously, in this atmosphere of sexual tension, physical beauty outpaces all other values and ideals. The girl who is unusually attractive has the world at her feet. The handsome, athletic boy is king of the mountain. The vast majority look in the mirror with disgust and disdain.

Any adolescent who wants to measure personal worth needs only to watch TV, play a video game, look at ads on billboards or in magazines, or see a music video. The message is clear: "If you're not beautiful, you don't matter." This is the brutal, one-point system that characterizes the competitive world of today's teenager.

To help understand the predicament facing our kids, suppose you are an adolescent girl, aged sixteen, named Holly Highschool. To be very honest, you are not exactly gorgeous. Your shoulders are rounded, and you have trouble remembering to close your mouth when you're thinking. That seems to worry your folks a lot. Pimples are distributed at random over your forehead and chin, and your oversized ears keep peeking out from under the hair that should hide them. You think often about these flaws and have wondered, with proper reverence, why God wasn't paying attention when you were being assembled.

You have never had a real date, except for that disaster last February. Your mom's friend, Mrs. Nosgood, arranged a blind date that almost signaled the end of the world. You knew it was risky to accept, but you were too excited to think rationally. Charming Chad arrived in high spirits, expecting to meet the girl of his dreams. You were not what he had in mind. Remember the disappointment on his face when you shuffled into the living room? Remember how he told Carrie the next day that you had so much bridgework in your mouth he'd have to pay a toll to kiss you? Horrible!

But the night of your date he didn't say anything. He just sulked through the evening and brought you home two hours early. Carrie couldn't wait to tell you the following afternoon how much Chad hated you, of course. You lashed back in anger. You caught him in the hall and told him he wasn't too bright for a boy with a head shaped like a light-bulb. But the hurt went deep. You despised all males for at least six months and thought your hormones would never make a comeback.

When you arrived home from school that afternoon, you went straight to your room without speaking to the family. You closed the door and sat on the bed. You thought about the injustice of it all, letting your young mind play hopscotch over many painful little memories that refused to fade. In fact, it seemed as though you were suddenly on trial to determine your acceptability to the human race.

The attorney for the prosecution stands before the jury to present incriminating evidence of your unworthiness. He recalls the fourth-grade Valentine's Day party when your beautiful cousin, Ann, got thirty-four cards and two boxes of candy, mostly from lovesick boys. You got three cards—two from girls and one from your uncle Albert in San Antonio. The jury shakes their heads in sorrow. The next evidence is that sixth-grade boy who shared his ice-cream cone with Betsy Brigden but said he'd "catch the uglies" if you took a bite. You acted as if you didn't hear, but you went to the girls' restroom and cried until recess was over.

"Ladies and gentlemen of the jury, these are unbiased opinions from Holly's own generation," the prosecutor summarizes. "The entire student body of Washington High School obviously agrees. They have no reason to lie. This homely girl simply does not deserve to be one of us! I urge you to find her guilty."

The attorney for the defense rises, a frail little man who stutters. He presents a few witnesses on your behalf, Mom and Dad—and Uncle Albert, of course.

"Objection, your honor!" shouts the prosecutor. "These are members of her family. They don't count. They're biased witnesses, and their opinions are untrustworthy."

"Objection sustained," mumbles the bored judge.

Your attorney, obviously flustered that the witnesses have been discounted, mentions that you have kept your room clean and makes a big deal about that "A" you got on a geography test last month. The foreman of the jury suppresses a yawn.

"A-a-and ssso, l-l-ladies and gentlemen of the j-jury, I ask y-y-you to find this y-young lady in-innocent of the charges."

The jury is gone about thirty-seven seconds before returning their verdict. You stand before them all—last year's homecoming queen, the quarterback of the football team, the senior class valedictorian, and the surgeon's handsome son. They all look down at you with stern eyes and shout in one voice: "Guilty as charged, your honor!" The judge immediately pronounces sentence: "Holly Highschool, a jury of your peers has found you to be unacceptable to the human race. You are hereby sentenced to a life of loneliness. You will probably fail in everything you do, and you'll go to your grave without a friend in the world. Marriage is out of the question, and there will never be a child in your home. You are a failure, Holly. You're a disappointment to your parents and must be considered excess baggage from this point forward. This case is closed."

The dream faded, but the decision of the jury remained all too real. Your parents wondered why you were so irritable during the following weeks. They never knew—and you didn't tell them—that you had been expelled from the world of the beautiful people.

I wish I could talk to all the Hollys and Robs and Sarahs and Mikes who have been found unacceptable in the courtroom of the mind. They need to know that the trial was rigged, that every member of the jury had been charged with the same offense, and that the judge was convicted thirty years ago. We have all stood before that bar of injustice, and few have been acquitted. Some of the adolescent convicts will be "pardoned" later in life, but a greater number always accept the sentence. And the irony of it all is that we each conduct our own rigged trial. We serve as our own prosecutor, and the final sentence is imposed under our own inflexible supervision—with a little help from our "friends," of course.

Beauty and the Adult

I am sitting at this moment near the guest swimming pool of the Sheraton Hotel, Waikiki Beach, Honolulu, Hawaii (if one must write, he may as well enjoy the process). The beautiful pool is virtually deserted, although around its borders lie several hundred narcissistic body-worshipers. They are a curious lot, when one stops to examine them. Each clutches a bottle of suntan lotion and rotates the flesh systematically under the burning sun—giant rotisseries, baking themselves evenly on all sides. They endure this monotonous activity for hours, checking their color regularly and comparing their skin tone with those around them. Medical science tells them this solar exposure will wrinkle them like prunes within a few years, and they will likely develop skin cancers late in life. No matter. They are in hot pursuit of instant beauty, and it is worth the cost.

But all is not well among the older set. In addition to the physical worries of children and teenagers, we adults have another formidable enemy: aging! It is said that time is not a thief—it is an embezzler, juggling the books at night so we won't notice anything is missing. Then suddenly, at about thirty years of age, Mr. Young begins to realize that everything is gradually turning loose. He presses his face close to the mirror and examines signs of deterioration. He's been hit by the well-known triple threat: sag, wrinkle, and droop! The pull of gravity is steadily destroying his jawline, and there is no way to anchor it into place. Most of the musculature that once rippled across his chest has melted and skidded down toward his protruding stomach. A little more of his precious hair defects to the pillow each night, eventually leaving nothing above his ears but skin and bone.

His wife can hardly console him, for she has troubles of her own. She brags to her husband that she still has the body of a twenty-year-old, and he replies, "Well, give it back. You're getting it all wrinkled." The middle-aged woman who still has her "schoolgirl figure" was probably a pretty dumpy kid. Such jokes strike home. In her panic to preserve what is left, she rushes to the pharmacist to buy seaweed extract or the latest herbal compound—anything that promises to tighten, mask, and undergird that which is sliding. Alas, her careful reconstruction washes off each evening, leaving the same old grooves and lines and bags and bumps. She then bakes in the sun and jiggles in the gym, but nothing helps for long. Obviously this inevitable process of aging is extremely painful for a beauty worshiper, whether masculine or feminine.

Having tried everything else, American women rush to their plastic surgeons, enduring considerable pain and expense to roll back the years. American doctors perform cosmetic surgery more than a half million times each year—liposuction, breast augmentation, nose jobs, face-lifts, and tummy tucks. Surprisingly, research shows that at least half the working women who get a face-lift can expect to receive salary increases in the months that follow. It is clear that beauty is a marketable commodity in the business world. Most bosses seek attractive secretaries and receptionists, whereas homely women often find it difficult to obtain a job of any kind.

At least half the working women who get a face–lift can expect to receive salary increases in the months that follow.

Most of the major choices made by adults are influenced one way or another by the attribute of beauty. A half-inch of flesh on the end of a woman's nose, for example, would likely rearrange her entire life, particularly affecting her selection of (or by) a marital partner. Each of us possesses a certain amount of physical bargaining power for use in romantic ventures, and most men attempt to "capture" a mate with the greatest possible beauty. A very attractive spouse is a highly desirable prize to be displayed.

Unattractive men do not escape the discrimination. Ugly salesmen are less successful than their handsome competitors. Homely politicians are asked to kiss fewer babies—and we all know what that means on election day. But perhaps the most common form of masculine discrimination is directed against the short man, who faces lifelong disadvantages. It is interesting to note that in all but three presidential elections since 1900 the taller candidate has won. Coolidge in 1924, Nixon in 1972, and Carter in 1976 were the shorter exceptions to this rule (and some would say they should have lost, but I'll leave that up to you).

Adults are hardly immune to the tyranny of the beauty cult, though they're old enough to know better. After Richard Speck viciously murdered eight nurses in their Chicago apartment during the late 1960s, one newsman remarked, "The thing that makes this tragedy much worse is that all eight of these girls were so attractive!" If beauty made these girls more valuable human beings, then the opposite premise must also be true: The murders would have been less tragic if the dead girls had been homely.

The conclusion, as written by George Orwell, is inescapable: "All [people] are equal, but some [people] are more equal than others."[7]

Beauty and the Elderly

As the baby-boomer generation grays, these architects of the "young-is-beautiful" era are getting a taste of the full implications of being the unwanted generation in a world dominated by the young. To become aged is to be unable to see or hear well, to have an active mind hopelessly trapped in an incapacitated body, to become dependent on busy children, to face increased difficulties with sexuality in an eroticized society, to be less able to contribute things that are deemed really worthwhile, to have few or no peers who share memories of younger days. This is inferiority at its worst. As stated in the first chapter, I am certain that many physical illnesses of old age are triggered by feelings of worthlessness. A gastroenterologist (specializing in stomach and intestinal problems) told me that 80 percent of his older patients have physical symptoms caused by emotional problems. They feel unneeded and unloved, and their despair is quickly translated into bodily disorders. Obviously, love and esteem are essential to humans of all ages.

Conclusion

I have not written the preceding description to discourage parents. There is much room for hope and optimism for the family that acts to counterbalance these harmful forces on behalf of their children. However, in the second half of the twentieth century the tendency among North American and Western European parents has been to "farm out" more and more elements of parental responsibility. We ask the child-care center, the preschool, the elementary educators, and the church to assume many of the instructional tasks previously handled by the family.

A popular theme in recent literature has been "How to be a good parent in your spare time." This notion assumes that effective child rearing is duck soup for the parent who organizes and delegates properly. But the building of self-esteem in your child is one responsibility that cannot be delegated. The task is too difficult and too personal to be handled in group situations. Without your commitment and support, a child stands unarmed against formidable foes. With few exceptions, our materialistic society is not going to reinforce healthy self-concepts in your children. If these desirable attitudes are to be constructed, only you can do it. It is both simplistic and dangerous to lock step with the attitude of one 1990s book that it "takes a village" to raise a child. Solid self-worth depends far more on the family than anyone else. No one else will care enough to make the necessary investment. This book is devoted to helping parents and teachers achieve that objective.

Questions and Answers

Why do people seem to be more conscious of their physical flaws and inadequacies now than in the past? What accounts for the "epidemic" of inferiority you describe?

In addition to the influence of the entertainment industry mentioned earlier, I believe this tremendous emphasis on physical attractiveness is a by-product of the sexual revolution. Our society has been erotically supercharged since the mid-1960s, when the traditional moral standards and restraints began to collapse. Television, radio, magazines, movies, billboards, literature, and clothing all reflect this unparalleled fascination with sensuality. When sex becomes all-important, obviously sex appeal and charm take on added social significance. The more steamed up a culture becomes over sex, the more it rewards beauty and punishes ugliness.

The need to be sexually attractive has become so powerful in America today that each person is expected to maximize his or her own seductiveness. When in our history have so many women spent their paychecks on tanning salons or face-lifts or had their hair professionally maintained each week? Some men and women even try to manufacture their beauty marks in a tattoo parlor. When have so many children struggled to find the right hairstyle? These factors reflect social pressure of the highest magnitude. Women, particularly, are urged by a billion-dollar beauty industry to conceal their physical flaws and reveal almost everything else, regardless of cost.

I have always enjoyed "people watching" on a busy sidewalk, noting how diligent each passerby is with exterior maintenance. Some faces must take hours to assemble before the mirror, particularly if "Mother Nature" did a sloppy job in the beginning. I have known one vain physician, for example, who was almost totally bald, but his patients never suspected it. He retained a patch of hair around the ears and neck to ten or more inches in length. Each morning the self-conscious doctor weaved it all together on the top of his head and glued it down with hair spray. He obviously knew that bald-headed doctors are "seen" differently than hairy ones—and hairy is better.

During a visit to Europe I looked for evidence of the same body awareness among the natives, but it was not as apparent. The women were no less attractive than American women, but they had obviously not invested the same effort in perfecting their physical endowments. American marketing efforts have had their impact on even the poorest countries of the former USSR, however. In the 1990s these countries became an exploding market for beauty products and designer jeans costing many days' labor each.

Any advertiser knows that sex and beauty remain the sensitive nerves on which to romp. Subtly or with the finesse of a call girl, marketing companies connect these motivations to their products. We've been sold toothpaste that fights tartar and grants sex appeal (how foolish!), breakfast cereal that makes us better looking (let's have a bowl), and mints that guarantee a second kiss. If we wear the right jeans, drink the right diet soda, and drive the right sports car, we will be svelte and sexy, strongly desirable. So the ads say. So Robin said to Batman about the batmobile in one of their 1990s movies: "It's the car. Chicks dig the car." There is no way to estimate the number of dollars spent each year to make us more competitive in an eroticized society.

It is my view that the sensuality that has been building in North America and Westernized societies generally from the 1960s has generated a higher incidence of emotional casualties among people who are intensely aware of their inability to compete in the flirtatious game. If beauty represents the necessary currency, the gold coin of worth, they are undeniably bankrupt. Sadly, the most vulnerable victims of this foolish measure of human worth are the little children who are too young to understand, too immature to compensate, and too crushed to fight back.

What are the prospects for the very pretty or handsome child? Does this child look forward to smooth sailing all the way?

This child has some remarkable advantages in self-acceptance and self-confidence. However, some problems also lie ahead that most homely children will never experience. Beauty in our society is power, and power can be dangerous in immature hands. A fourteen-year-old who is prematurely curved and rounded in all the right places will be pursued vigorously by males who would exploit her beauty. As she becomes more conscious of her flirtatious power, she is sometimes urged toward early promiscuity. Furthermore, women who have been coveted physically since early childhood may become bitter and disillusioned by the depersonalization of body worship.

Research also indicates some interesting consequences in regard to marital stability for the "beautiful people." In one important study, the more attractive college girls were found to be less happily married twenty-five years later. It is apparently difficult to reserve the "power" of sex for one mate, ignoring the ego gratification that awaits outside the marriage bonds. Finally, the more attractive a person in youth, the more painful the aging process becomes.

My point is this: The measurement of worth on a scale of beauty is wrong, often damaging both the "haves" and the "have-nots."

3

Intelligence

The Silver Coin of Human Worth

Intelligence is another extremely critical attribute in evaluating the worth of a child, second only to beauty in its importance. These two qualities are not merely desirable features that we hope our children will possess; they rank at the very top of our value system, above every imaginable alternative. When either characteristic is missing in a child, parents often experience the agony, guilt, and disappointment of having produced an inferior child, a creation with the same intolerable flaws they have long despised in themselves. When the birth of a firstborn is imminent, parents pray for a normal baby—that is, "average." But from that moment on, average will not be good enough.

The Parental View

Shortly after examining their baby's eyes, ears, nose, and related appendages for imperfections, most new parents begin looking for the signs of budding genius. And they seem to find them. A child's growth and development are so rapid during the first year of life that awestruck parents watch their "brilliant" creation in amazement. "Only eight months ago the kid was completely helpless; now look at him! He said 'Mama' six full weeks before the average child; this kid's got a real head on his shoulders." They give him credit for having smiled at five days of age when in reality "the kid" was grimacing from a severe gas pain.

As their child steamrolls into the second year of life, evidence mounts that he is intellectually loaded. What his parents may not know is that human mental awakening is thrilling to watch, even in the average youngster. Every day, it seems, something new is learned or mimicked. This normal process is terribly exciting to those who are watching for the first time. How many parents have said to me with blatant pride: "You wouldn't believe how that boy can think and reason. He remembers things I told him weeks ago." They estimate his IQ to be somewhere between 180 and 240, depending on his willingness to cooperate. They start saving money for his college education.

Then come the "terrible twos," when Junior learns the meaning of one word much better than all others— "No!" He is impossible to handle and wants his own way in everything. His parents find him a pain and a trial, but they are secretly proud that he is going to be an independent thinker and a leader. "Look how he pushes the other children around. This kid isn't going to be a follower; you can sure see that!"

Time will prove, however, that Junior's parents have drawn some premature and unwarranted conclusions. As he reaches his third, fourth, and fifth birthdays, he appears less and less remarkable. Mom and Dad begin to have some nagging doubts about the new genius in their family. In fact, much of his behavior seems depressingly ordinary. He is often giddy, noisy, and characteristically childish. He would much rather play than work, and he has still not learned to read. At last he skips off to kindergarten, and the golden image of the "superchild" suddenly turns green.

The first "open house" night is a devastating experience for Junior's loving parents. They are tense as cats when they arrive at school, facing the unknown verdict. For six weeks their pudgy little pride-and-joy has been out there beyond reach. *What* has he been doing? Whether they admit it or not, their reputation as "good parents" is on the line. If Junior has been a brat, their discipline is faulty. If he has refused to work, they are guilty of teaching him irresponsibility. But it is worse if he appears dumb, for they must have endowed him with inferior mental equipment. Their egos are inextricably wrapped around this firstborn child; his mistakes, failures, and blunders send barbed arrows into their backsides.

The parents glance quickly around the classroom to the place where children's work is exhibited, but Junior's paper isn't there. Then they see it, down in the lower corner of the bulletin board, very near the floor. It is awful! They blush at the unbelievably sloppy mess. That couldn't be his! But it has his misspelled name on it. Just then Miss Dingle comes over to meet Junior's parents. She is pleasant and professional, smiling and winking and explaining her program. They nervously ask how Junior is doing, and she hangs a two-second pause that is pregnant with meaning. "Well," Miss Dingle begins, "I've been intending to get in touch with you."

Not all parents overestimate the intellectual potential of their children, as did Junior's parents. Some experience tremendous anxiety over their child's early slowness and immaturity. They have memorized the average ages at which children typically learn to sit up, crawl, eat with a spoon, say "da da," and throw string beans, and they know that their little one is behind in too many areas. The unspeakable fear of mental retardation hovers over them day by day, and they await each developmental milestone with unconcealed tension.

Whether parents overestimate or underestimate the mental potential of their children, it is obvious that most of them are highly sensitive and vulnerable regarding intelligence. Therefore, it is appropriate to ask why so much tension is associated with the brain power of the next generation.

I talked recently with a family that applied for the adoption of a child. They had finally received the long-awaited telephone call informing them that a baby had been selected for their consideration. The father told me how he questioned the representative from the adoption agency about the infant's history and heritage:

- "Did the baby's mother use drugs during pregnancy?"
- "How intelligent are the parents?"
- "How tall are they?"
- "How well did they do in school?"
- "What do they look like?"

- "Is any hereditary disease evident in their medical histories?"
- "How long did labor last?"
- "What did the obstetrician say in his report?"
- "Has the child been seen by a pediatrician?"

During the course of this intense questioning, the father began to feel guilty about his motives: "I realized I was inspecting and evaluating this child as if I were buying a new automobile. I was actually asking if this baby boy was 'qualified' to become my son. I suddenly comprehended that the infant lying there before me was a magnificent human being, regardless of any flaws and disadvantages. He was the creation of God, who had given him an immortal soul, yet there I stood demanding a perfect child who could become a personal credit to me."

This father's attitude toward his adopted child is observed frequently in the reaction of natural parents as well. Their child must excel; must succeed; must triumph; must be the first of that age to walk, talk, or ride a tricycle; must earn a stunning report card and be chosen for the "gifted and talented" educational program. Mom and Dad want a bumper sticker that says "My child was student of the month at Albert Einstein Elementary School." This superchild must star in Little League; must be the quarterback or homecoming queen or senior class president or valedictorian; must be a cheerleader or forensics competition medalist or soloist. Throughout the formative years of childhood, parents give their child the same message: "We're counting on you to do something fantastic. Now don't disappoint us!"

According to Martha Weinman Lear, author of *The Child Worshippers*, the younger generation is our most reliable status symbol. Middle-class parents vigorously compete with each other in raising the best-dressed, best-fed, best-educated, best-mannered, best-medicated, best-cultured, and best-adjusted child on the block. The hopes, dreams, and ambitions of an entire family sometimes rest on the shoulders of an immature child. And in this atmosphere of fierce competition, the parent who produces an intellectually gifted child is clearly holding the winning sweepstakes ticket.

Unfortunately, exceptional children are just that—exceptions. Seldom does a five-year-old memorize the Bible, play chess blindfolded, or compose symphonies in the Mozart manner. To the contrary, the vast majority of children are not dazzlingly brilliant, extremely witty, highly coordinated, tremendously talented, or universally popular. And if they are candid, the parents of a child who does rank in the "exceptional" category in some area will admit to having their own serious problems guiding their youngster through life. Fortunately, the average child is "average," with oversized needs to be loved and accepted as is. Without that acceptance, the stage is set for unrealistic pressure on the younger generation and considerable disappointment for their parents.

The Child's View

As stated in chapter 1, children understand the importance of physical attractiveness by the time they are three or four years of age. Every conceivable educational resource is mobilized to drill home the necessity of "looking good." The second essential human attribute, intelligence, is much more subtle in its impact. A child with low to average ability does not have his IQ tattooed on his forehead and often survives the preschool years with self-respect intact. He may be five or six years old before he notices the vast differences between himself and his brighter friends. Then it happens! He begins his school career, and the whole world cracks and splinters in slow motion.

Make no mistake about it: School is a dangerous place for children with fragile egos. For the slow child, the typical setting is unintentionally programmed to disassemble self-confidence, bit by bit, until nothing remains but broken pieces. Having been a teacher, I am well acquainted with the many ways self-esteem is innocently assaulted in the classroom.

> *For the slow child, [school] is unintentionally programmed to disassemble self-confidence, bit by bit, until nothing remains but broken pieces.*

Miss Lodestar announces to her students that they are going to have a math contest. The ever-popular Matt and Katie are asked to serve as captains, choosing team members alternately. Katie is granted first-draft choice, and she grabs the ranking intellectual superstar, who moves to the side of the room nearest the captain. Matt's first choice also goes to a kid with exceptional brain power. Through this entire process, Arnie is slumped down in his seat, knowing trouble is coming. He's thinking, *Somebody take me!* But Arnie can't even read—much less do math—and everyone knows he's stupid. The captains go on choosing until there's nobody left in the center of the room except Arnie. Matt says, "You take him," and Katie says, "No! You take him." Finally Miss Lodestar orders Matt to include Arnie on his team. And sure enough, when the contest begins, who flubs up? Who causes his team to lose? Who wishes he could curl up and die?

Arnie's learning problem is one of five common academic difficulties, each leading its victim to believe he or she is stupid—and, of course, unworthy. These five may be illustrated as:

1. *The slow learner.* Arnie, the child described above, is a slow learner—a very slow learner. No one knows why, least of all Arnie. He tries to do the work, but nothing turns out right. He can't read. He doesn't understand science. He rarely receives a "happy face" for doing things properly, and *never* has his teacher written "Nice work, Arnie" on his paper. He is the only child in the room who won't get a gold star on his spelling chart. Does all this bad news escape Arnie's observation? Certainly not! He isn't *that* slow. How foolish he feels! There is no explanation he can offer. He is utterly defenseless. He must sit there in front of everybody and fail, day after day. Consequently, something precious is dying inside Arnie. Oh, he'll go on living, but the youthful enthusiasm and excitement will soon be extinguished. Several decades from now people will wonder why Arnie is such an uncreative, insecure bore. And no one will be there to tell them that his light went out when he was six years old.

2. *The semiliterate child.* Martha is a seven-year-old Hispanic-American girl who is repeating first grade. She is semiliterate, a problem often erroneously called "bilingual." Two languages are spoken in her home, but she has learned neither of them very well. She is confused and feels incapable of expressing herself. She feels incredibly stupid. That is why she

never makes a sound unless utterly compelled to talk. Silence is her only defense against the hostile world around her.

3. *The underachiever.* Sherrie is a bright young lady. Intelligence test results place her within the upper 10 percent of her classmates, and she can handle most academic tasks with ease. Unfortunately, Sherrie is not very disciplined. She is easily distracted, frequently bored, and seldom motivated. She does her work as quickly as possible, just to get it finished, and avoids any unnecessary effort. Homework is out of the question, so she effectively conceals from her parents what has been assigned. Every attempt to get Sherrie moving is followed by yet another burst of inertia. Furthermore, she doesn't *know* she is bright. The comments on her work papers give no clue as to her ability, since they merely reflect her sloppiness and inaccuracy. Her parents and teacher are obviously displeased with her performance, and Sherrie is likely to draw the same conclusion as her less able friends: "I am dumb!" She may turn out to have Attention Deficit Disorder (ADD) or Attention Deficit Hyperactive Disorder (ADHD). A child developmentalist or a physician should be asked to assess Sherrie's situation.

4. *The culturally deprived child.* Willie is a child from an impoverished neighborhood. He has never visited a zoo or ridden on a plane or been fishing. His daddy's identity is a mystery, and his mother works long hours to support five little children. His vocabulary is minuscule, except for an astounding array of slang words. He has no place to read or study at home. Willie *knows* he isn't going to make it in school, and this fact already influences his personal evaluation.

5. *The late bloomer.* Finally, I want you to meet Donald, who is a "late bloomer." To understand his story, we must

return to his preschool days. The following section is from my book, *Dare to Discipline*:

Donald is five years old and will soon go to kindergarten. He is an immature little fellow who still is his mamma's baby in many ways. Compared to his friends, Donald's language is childish, and his physical coordination is gross. He cries three or four times a day, and other children take advantage of his innocence. A developmental psychologist or pediatrician would verify that Donald is neither physically ill nor mentally retarded; he is merely progressing on a slower physiological time-table than most children his age. Nevertheless, Donald's fifth birthday has arrived, and everyone knows that middle-class five-year-olds go to kindergarten. He is looking forward to school, but deep inside he is rather tense about this new challenge. He knows his mother is anxious for him to do well in school, although he doesn't really know why. His father has told him he will be a "failure" if he doesn't get a good education. He's not certain what a failure is, but he sure doesn't want to be one. Mom and Dad are expecting something outstanding from him and he hopes he won't disappoint them. His sister Pamela is in the second grade now; she is doing well. She can read and print her letters and she knows the names of every day in the week. Donald hopes he will learn those things too.

Kindergarten proves to be tranquil for Donald. He rides the tricycle and pulls the wagon and plays with the toy clock. He prefers to play alone for long periods of time, providing his teacher, Miss Moss, is nearby. It is clear to Miss Moss that Donald is immature and unready for the first grade, and she talks to his parents about the possibility of delaying him for a year. "Flunk kindergarten?!" says his father. "How can the kid flunk kindergarten?" Miss Moss tried to explain that Donald has not failed kindergarten; he merely needs another year to develop before entering the first grade. The suggestion sends his father into a glandular upheaval. "The kid is six years old; he should be learning to read and write. What good is it doing him to drag around that dumb wagon and ride on a stupid tricycle? Get the kid in the first grade!" Miss Moss and her principal reluctantly comply.

The following September Donald clutches his Mickey Mouse lunch pail and walks on wobbly legs to the first grade. From day one he begins to have academic trouble, and reading seems to be his biggest source of difficulty. His new teacher, Miss Fudge, introduces the alphabet to her class, and Donald realizes that most of his friends have already learned it. He has a little catching up to do. But too quickly Miss Fudge begins teaching something new; she wants the class to learn the sounds each letter represents, and soon he is even further behind. Before long, the class begins to read about Dick and Jane and their immortal dog "Spot." Some children can zing right along, but Donald is still working on the alphabet. Miss Fudge divides the class into three reading groups according to their initial skill. She wants to conceal the fact that one group is doing more poorly than the others, so she gives the camouflage names of "Lions," "Tigers," and "Giraffes." Miss Fudge's motive is noble, but she fools no one. It takes the students about two minutes to realize that the Giraffes are all stupid! Donald begins to worry about his lack of progress, and the gnawing thought looms that there may be something drastically wrong with him.

During the first parent-teacher conference in October, Miss Fudge tells Donald's parents about his problems in school. She describes his immaturity and his inability to concentrate or sit still in the classroom. "Nonsense," says his father. "What the kid needs is a little drill." He insists that Donald bring him his books, allowing father and son to sit down for an extended academic exercise. But everything Donald does irritates his father. His childish mind wanders and he forgets the things he was told five minutes before. As his father's tension mounts, Donald's productivity descends. At one point, Donald's father crashes his hand on the table and calls his son "Stupid!" The child will never forget that knifing assessment.

Whereas Donald struggled vainly to learn during his early days in school, by November he has become disinterested and unmotivated. He looks out the window. He draws and doodles with his pencil. He whispers and plays. Since he can't read, he can neither spell, nor write, nor do his social studies. He is uninvolved and bored, not knowing what is going on most of the time. He feels fantastically inferior and inadequate. "Please stand, Donald, and read the next paragraph," says his teacher. He stands and shifts his weight from foot to foot as he struggles to identify the first word. The girls snicker and he hears one of the boys say, "What a dummy!" The problem began as a developmental lag, but has now become an emotional time bomb and a growing hatred for school.[1]

The categories of learning problems I've described (slow learner, semiliterate, underachiever, culturally deprived, and late bloomer) represent the five large groups of students who consistently fail in the classroom. It is appalling to recognize that the children in these five categories actually outnumber those students who feel successful in school! This means that personal dissatisfaction and disappointment are common products of our educational system. It accounts for the large percentage of adults who secretly "know" they are stupid— the lesson they learned best during their school days.

As stated earlier, if we are to understand our children— their feelings and behavior—then we must sharpen our memories of our own childhood. Can you recall the agonizing moments when you felt incredibly dumb as a child? Can

A child can lose confidence in a thousand ways, and the reconstruction of personal worth is usually a slow, difficult process.

you feel, even today, the rush of hot blood to your ears and neck when you blundered into a social mistake? Do you remember withering under a deafening guffaw after you said something foolish at school? Is it possible to feel, one more time, the sting of ridicule and disrespect from the whole world? Every child experiences uncomfortable moments like these, but alas, some

youngsters live with disgrace every day of their lives. The child with less than average ability is often predestined for this maelstrom of despair.

Other Components of Confidence

I have emphasized the critical importance of two factors, beauty and intelligence, in shaping self-esteem and confidence. For men, physical attractiveness gradually submerges as a value during late adolescence and early adulthood, yielding first place to intelligence. For women, however, beauty retains its number-one position even into middle age and beyond. The reason the average woman would rather have beauty than brains is because she believes the average man can see better than he can think. Her value system is based on his and will probably continue that way. A man's personal preferences are also rooted in the opinions of the opposite sex, since most women value intelligence in men over attractive physical arrangement.

Certainly beauty and intelligence are not the only ingredients in self-esteem. We have all known attractive intellectuals who could not conceal their own personal dissatisfaction. My point has been, simply, that inferiority is most often related to these two important values. Other common influences are evident as well.

- *Parents* have a remarkable power to preserve or damage the self-worth of a child. Their manner either conveys respect and love or disappointment and disinterest. This parental role is discussed in greater detail in the strategies described in later chapters.

- *Older siblings* can crush the confidence of a younger, weaker child. The little one can never run as fast, or fight as well, or achieve as much as big brother and sister. And if their words are perpetual scorn, a younger child can easily feel foolish and incapable.

- *Early social blunders and mistakes* are sometimes extremely painful, even when remembered throughout adulthood.

- *Financial hardship*, depriving a child of clothes and lifestyle of peers, can cause a child to feel inferior. It is not the poverty that does the damage. Rather, it is the relative comparison with others. It is possible to feel deprived when you are truly rich by the world's standards. Incidentally, money is probably the third most important source of self-esteem in our culture. In the materialistic eyes of society, for example, a pimply faced teenager on a bicycle is somehow less worthy than a pimply faced teenager in a Nissan.

- *Disease*, even when unapparent, may represent the child's "inner flaw." A cardiac condition that forces Mom to nag and beg him to go slow can convince a child that he is brittle and defective.

- A child who has been raised in a *protected environment*, such as a farm or a foreign missionary outpost, may be embarrassed by undeveloped social skills and pull inward in shy withdrawal.

- *Embarrassing family characteristics*, such as an alcoholic father or a mentally challenged sibling, can produce feelings of inferiority through close identification with the disrespected relatives.

Unfortunately, this list could be almost endless. In working with the problem of inadequacy, I have drawn this conclusion: A child can lose confidence in a thousand ways, and the reconstruction of personal worth is usually a slow, difficult process.

Part 2

Strategies for Esteem

4

Build a Values–Safe Environment

It is high time that we declare all-out war on the destructive value system I have been describing—the system that reserves self-worth and dignity for a select minority. I reject the notion that inferiority and inadequacy are inevitable, that the present epidemic of self-doubt is unavoidable. Although our task is more difficult for some children than for others, there *are* ways to teach a child of his genuine significance, regardless of the shape of his nose or the size of his ears or the efficiency of his mind.

Every child is entitled to hold up his or her head, not in haughtiness, but in confidence and security. That is the concept of human worth intended by our Creator. How foolish for us to doubt our value when He formed us in His own image. His view of the beauty cult was made abundantly clear more than three thousand years ago when Samuel was seeking a king for Israel. Samuel naturally selected the tallest, handsomest son of Jesse, but God told him he had chosen the wrong man, saying: "Don't judge by a man's face or height, for this [David's brother] is not the one. I don't make decisions the way you do! Men judge by outward appearance, but I look at a man's thoughts and intentions" (1 Samuel 16:7 TLB). Despite the clarity of this message, we have not taught it to our children. Some of the little folk feel so inferior, they cannot believe even God could love them. They feel totally worthless and empty, thinking that God neither cares nor understands.

Chris was such a child. He wrote the following note to Dr. Richard A. Gardner, a psychotherapist who works with children:

> Dear Doctor Gardner
>
> What is bothering me is that long ago some big person it was a boy about 13 years old. He called me turtle and I know he said that because of my plastic sergery.
>
> And I think god hates me because of my lip. And when I die he'll probably send me to hell.
>
> Love, Chris

Can't you feel Chris's loneliness and despair? How unfortunate for a seven-year-old child to believe that he is already hated by the entire universe! What a waste of the potential that existed at the moment of his birth. What unnecessary pain he will bear throughout his lifetime. Yet Chris is merely one more victim of a stupid, inane system of evaluating human worth—a system that stresses attributes that cannot be obtained by the majority of our children. Instead of rewarding honesty, integrity, courage, loyalty, patience, diligence, or other virtues praised in earlier times, we reserve maximum credit for bright young people who "look good" on a beach. Isn't it now appropriate that we abandon this needless discrimination?

So what are we to do? How can we, as parents and teachers, build strong egos and indomitable spirits in our children, despite the prevailing social forces? What are the steps necessary to reverse the trend? The following suggestions and recommendations address these questions, offering specific strategies to be applied. These strategies focus on the early home life, the school years, the adolescent experience, and matters pertinent to adults. Each strategy is followed by a question-and-answer section reflecting actual requests for specific advice I have received from parents.

It has been my purpose to formulate a well-defined philosophy—an approach to child rearing—that will contribute to self-esteem from infancy onward.

Strategy 1: Examine the Values in Your Home

In a very real sense, we parents are products of the society whose values I have condemned. We have systematically been taught to worship beauty and brains, as has everyone else, including our grandmas and grandpas and uncles and aunts and cousins and neighbors. We all want superchildren who will amaze the world. Let's face it, folks: We have met the enemy, and he is us! Often the greatest damage is unintentionally inflicted in the home, which should be the child's sanctuary and fortress. Further, I have observed in working with parents that their *own* feelings of inferiority make it difficult for them to accept gross imperfections in their children. They don't intend to reject their sons and daughters. They work hard to conceal these inner thoughts. But their "damaged" child symbolizes their own inadequacies and failures. Thus, it takes a very mature parent to look into the eyes of an unattractive child, or one who is clearly deficient in mentality, and say, "Not only do I love you, little one, but I recognize your immeasurable worth as a human being."

Often the greatest damage is unintentionally inflicted in the home, which should be the child's sanctuary and fortress.

The first step in building your child's esteem, then, is to examine your own feelings—to even be willing to expose those heretofore unconscious guilt-laden attitudes. Are you secretly disappointed because your child is ordinary? Have you rejected her, at times, because she lacks appeal and charm? Do you think he is dumb and stupid? Was she born during a difficult time, imposing a financial and physical stress on the family? Did you want a girl instead of a boy or a boy instead of a girl? Was this child conceived out of wedlock, forcing an unwanted marriage? Do you resent the freedom you lost or the demands a child places on your time and effort? Does he embarrass you by being either too loud and rambunctious or too inward and withdrawn? You can't teach a child to respect himself when you dislike him for reasons of your own. By examining your innermost feelings, perhaps with the help of an understanding counselor or doctor, you *can* make room in your heart for your less-than-perfect youngster. After all, what right do we have to demand superchildren when we are so ordinary ourselves?

A sizable portion of your child's self-concept emerges from the way he thinks you "see" him. He watches what you say and do with interest. He is more alert to your "statements" regarding his worth than on any other subject. He even reads your unspoken (and perhaps unconscious) attitudes. Dr. Stanley Coopersmith, assistant professor of psychology at the University of California, conducted an exhaustive study of self-esteem (described more fully in strategy 6) and concluded that parents have a tremendous influence on their child's self-perception. They can either equip a young person with the confidence necessary to withstand social pressures, or they can leave this vulnerable person virtually defenseless. The difference is in the quality of their interaction. The child convinced of parental love and respect is inclined to accept worth as a person.

However, I have observed that many children know intuitively that they are loved by their parents, but they do not believe they are held in high esteem. These seemingly contradictory attitudes are not so uncommon in human relationships. A wife can love her alcoholic husband, yet disrespect what he has become. A child can conclude: "Sure they love me because I'm their child—I can see that I'm important to them. But they are not proud of me as a person. I'm a disappointment to them. I've let them down. I'm not turning out as they had hoped."

I reemphasize: It is very easy to convey love and disrespect at the same time. A child can know that you would actually give your life if required, yet your doubts about his or her worth as a person show through. You are tense when your child speaks to guests or outsiders. You butt in to explain what he was trying to say, or laugh nervously if the remarks sound foolish. When someone asks him a direct question, you interrupt and answer. You reveal your frustration when you are trying to comb his hair or make him "look nice" for an important event. He knows you think it is an impossible assignment. If he is to spend a weekday away from the family, you give him an extended lecture on how to avoid making a fool of himself. These subtle behaviors are signals to the child that you don't trust him with *your* image—that he must be supervised closely to avoid embarrassing the whole family. Disrespect can be read into your manner, though it is framed in genuine love. The love is a private thing between you, whereas confidence and admiration are "other" oriented, having social implications to those outside the family.

Loving your child, therefore, is only half the task of building self-esteem. The element of respect must be added to counterbalance the insults of society. Unless *somebody* believes in the child's worth, the world can be a cold and lonely place indeed. It is for this reason that I described the enormous threats to esteem in the first two chapters. I want each parent to see just what a child faces and the importance of preparation to meet critics head-on.

There are, I believe, four common barriers that cause a child to doubt personal worth, even when deeply loved. I suggest that the reader do some self-examination as we discuss these pitfalls.

Parental Insensitivity

If there is one lesson parents need to learn most urgently, it is to guard what they say in the presence of their children.

Many times, following a speaking engagement, I have been consulted by a parent regarding a particular problem her child is having. As Mom describes the gritty details, the object of all this conversation is standing about a yard behind her, listening to a candid recital of all his faults. I flinch when I hear a parent unintentionally disassemble esteem in this fashion. I took my son and daughter to a park during a break in my writing of this book. While there, an insensitive mother was talking to me about her six-year-old boy, Roger, who stood within hearing distance just a few feet away.

She spoke in Gatling-gun fashion: "He had a high fever when he was born, about 105 at least. The doctor couldn't do nothing to help him. He gave Roger the wrong kind of pills. Now Roger won't ever be the same. They say he has some brain damage now, and he don't learn too good in school."

If Roger were my son, his disability would be the very last thing I would let him hear me describe to a stranger. It was like saying, "This is my son, Roger. He's the dumb one—you know, there's something wrong with his brain." How imperceptive she was of her unfortunate son. Roger did not show shock. In fact, he didn't even look up. But you can bet he heard his mother, and his self-concept will always reflect what she said.

Surprisingly, it is not just insensitive parents who blunder into this kind of foolishness. I recently referred a bright nine-year-old boy to a neurologist because of severe learning problems. After giving the lad a thorough examination, the physician called in his parents and discussed the full details of the boy's "brain damage" in front of his wide-eyed little patient. How can we preserve self-esteem when we have totally lost touch with childhood ourselves? Don't we know they are listening to us? It is a wise adult who understands that self-esteem is the most fragile characteristic in human nature, and once broken, its reconstruction is more difficult than repairing Humpty-Dumpty.

Parental sensitivity should be especially sharp in regard to matters pertaining to physical attractiveness and intelligence. Those are the two primary "soft spots" where their children are most vulnerable. It is, of course, impossible to shut out this value system entirely, for it penetrates like termites through the walls. Consider how the importance of beauty is taught through the casual occurrences and conversations of each day:

- *Advertisement:* "You, too, can have gorgeous hair."
- *Mother:* "Mr. and Mrs. Martin sure have cute kids, don't they?"
- *Fairy stories:* "Then the ugly duckling sat down to cry."
- *Television:* "The *new* Miss America is . . ."
- *Relative:* "My, what a pretty little girl you've become."

The whole world seems organized to convey this one message to the younger set. While you can't shield your child from its impact, you don't have to add to it yourself. You can also screen out the most offensive television programs and help your child select good reading material.

Sensitivity is a vitally important skill for teachers as well. Dr. Clyde Narramore, author and psychologist, describes being in a classroom where a teacher wanted to convey the concepts of "small" versus "large." She selected the tiniest withdrawn fellow, who rarely made a sound, and instructed him to stand beside her at the front. "Small!" she said. "David is small." She then dismissed him and summoned the tallest girl in the class. "Large! Large! Sharon is very large!" said the teacher. Dr. Narramore said every child in the room could see David and Sharon blush in humiliation, but the teacher failed to notice. We cannot preserve the esteem of the next generation if our eyes are always aimed about twenty-four inches above their bowed heads.

Sensitivity is the key word. It means "tuning in" to the thoughts and feelings of our kids, listening to the cues they give us, and reacting appropriately to what we detect.

Fatigue and Time Pressure

Why do dedicated parents have to be reminded to be sensitive to the needs of their children? Shouldn't this be the natural expression of their love and concern? Yes, it should, but Mom and Dad have some problems of their own. They are pushed to the limits of their endurance by the pressure of time. Dad is holding down three jobs, and he huffs and puffs to keep up with it all. Mom never has a free minute either. Tomorrow night she is having eight guests for dinner, and since she works during the day, she only has this one evening to clean the house, go to the market, arrange the flowers for the centerpiece, and put the hem in the dress she will wear. Her "to do" list is three pages long, and she already has a splitting headache from it all. She pops the kids' supper into the microwave and hopes the troops will stay out of her hair.

At about 7 p.m. little Joshua tracks down his perspiring mother and says, "Look what I just drawed, Mom." She glances downward and says, "Uh huh," obviously thinking about something else. Ten minutes later Josh asks her to get him some juice. She complies but resents his intrusion. She is behind schedule, and her tension is mounting. Five minutes later he interrupts again, this time wanting her to reach a toy that sits on the top shelf of the closet. She stands looking down at him for a moment, then hurries down the hall to meet his demand, mumbling as she goes. But as she passes his bedroom door, she notices that he has spread his toys all over the floor and made a mess with the glue. Mom explodes. Her screams rattle Josh's teeth.

Does this drama sound familiar? "Routine panic" is a way of life. I conducted an inquiry among seventy-five middle-class, married women who were between twenty-five and thirty-five years of age. I asked them to indicate the sources of depression that most often send them into despair and gloom. Many common problems were revealed, including in-law conflicts, financial hardships, difficulties with children, sexual problems, and mood fluctuations associated with the menstrual cycle and physiological distress. But to my surprise, fatigue from time pressure was tagged as *the* most trouble-some source of depression by half the group; the other half ranked it a close second.

It is obvious that many families live on a kind of last-minute emergency schedule, making it impossible to meet the demands of their own overcommitments. Why do they do it? The women I surveyed admitted their dislike for the pace they kept, yet it has become a monster that defies containment. Faster and faster they run, jamming more and more activities into their hectic days. Even their recreation is marked by this breakneck pace. There was a time when a man didn't fret if he missed a stagecoach. He'd just catch it next month. Now someone who misses a section of a revolving door is thrown into despair!

Who is the inevitable loser in this breathless lifestyle? It's the little person who is leaning against the wall with hands stuffed in the pockets of his blue jeans. He misses his father during the long day and tags around after him at night, saying, "Play ball, Dad!" But Dad is pooped. Besides, he has a briefcase full of work to be done.

Mom promised to take him to the park this afternoon, but deadlines forced her to put in overtime at her job. The child gets the message: The folks are busy again. Might as well drift into the family room and watch two hours of cartoons and reruns on television.

Crowded lives produce fatigue, fatigue produces irritability, and irritability produces indifference. Indifference can be interpreted by the child as a lack of love and respect.

Children just don't fit into a "to do" list very well. It takes time to be an effective parent when children are small. It takes time to introduce them to good books. It takes time to fly kites and play ball and put together jigsaw puzzles. It takes time to listen, once more, to the skinned-knee episode and talk about the bird with the broken wing. These building blocks of esteem, held together with the mortar of love, seldom materialize amidst busy timetables. Instead, crowded lives produce fatigue, fatigue produces irritability, and irritability produces indifference. Indifference can be interpreted by the child as a lack of love and respect.

Slow down, parents! Your children will be gone so quickly, and you will have nothing but blurred memories of those years when they needed you. I'm not suggesting that we invest our entire adult lives in the next generation, nor must everyone become parents. But once those children are here they had better fit into our schedules somewhere. Children can't raise themselves, and parents who have busy careers must find a way to work their boys and girls into their schedules.

Guilt

In case you haven't noticed, parenthood is a very guilt-producing affair—even for the dedicated "professional." The conflict of interest between the needs of children and the demands of adult responsibilities, as described above, is only one of many inconsistencies that strike pangs of guilt in our hearts. It is interesting to me that the situation gradually reverses itself. As parents age, grown children sometimes feel guilty over their failure to meet the needs of their aging parents. Since no one can parent perfectly, we subject ourselves to a constant cross-examination in the courtroom of parental acceptability. Was I fair in my discipline? Did I overreact out of frustration and anger? Have I been partial to the child who is my favorite? Did I cause that illness by giving poor care? Was the accident my fault? Have I made the same mistakes for which I resented my own parents? 'Round and 'round go the self-doubts and recriminations.

I have seen parents agonize over circumstances totally beyond their control, as when they give birth to a mentally or physically disabled child. Although the cause of the child's defect was genetic and completely unknowable until it occurred, they often interpret the disaster as punishment for some past sin. Once the idea has been accepted as truth, they will bear the personal responsibility for their child's misfortune from that day forward. This unfounded guilt can drive a wedge between two happily married people, destroying their relationship and consuming them in bitterness.

Guilt can interfere with a healthy parent-child relationship in numerous ways. First, it can take the joy out of parenthood, turning the entire responsibility into a painful chore. Second, guilt almost always affects the way a parent handles a child; the typical reaction is to buy everything Junior screams for, whether needed or not, and to become much too permissive in matters of control. The reasoning seems to be, "With all that I have done wrong, the least I can do for the child is avoid punishment and unpleasantness." As we will discuss later, self-esteem splinters under that freewheeling environment. Third, through some mystery of perception, a child can usually "feel" hidden guilt in parents. The child knows something unidentifiable is there and wonders about its meaning, possibly concluding that it is "all my fault." Guilt can be another formidable barrier in building self-respect among the young.

The best way to handle guilt is to face it squarely, using it to motivate change, where warranted. Dr. William Glasser, psychologist and author of *Reality Therapy*, said that guilt is a valuable emotion, providing the energy to improve and grow. Thus, I would suggest that "guilty" parents sit down together and discuss their personal dissatisfaction. They should actually write down their most troubling parental shortcomings and then assess each item.

- "Is my guilt valid?"
- "Can I do anything about it? If so, how?"

- "If I can do nothing about it, isn't it appropriate that I lay the matter to rest?"

Remember again that none of us can be perfect parents, any more than we can be perfect human beings. We get tired and frustrated and disappointed and irritable, affecting the way we approach those little ones around our feet. But fortunately, we are permitted to make many mistakes through the years—provided the overall tone is somewhere near the right note.

Rivals for Love

My son arrived on the scene when his sister was five years old. She had been the only granddaughter on either side of the family and had received all the adult attention that can be heaped upon a child. Suddenly, her secure kingdom was invaded by a cute little fellow who captured and held center stage. All of the relatives cuddled, cooed, rocked, bounced, and hugged baby Ryan, while Danae watched suspiciously from the wings. As we drove home from Grandmother's house on a Sunday afternoon, about a week after Ryan's arrival, my daughter suddenly said, "Daddy, you know I'm just talking. You know I don't mean to be bad or anything. But sometimes I wish little Ryan wasn't here."

She had given us a valuable clue to her feelings in that brief sentence, and we immediately seized the opportunity she had provided. We moved her into the front seat of the car so we could discuss what she had said. We told her we understood how she felt and assured her of our love. We also explained that a baby is completely helpless and will die if

88

people don't take care of him—feed, clothe, change, and love him. We reminded her that she was taken care of that way when she was a baby. Ryan would soon grow up too. We were also careful in the months that followed to minimize the threat to her place in our hearts. By giving careful attention to her feelings and security, the relationship with her brother developed into a lasting friendship and love.

Danae's admission was not a typical response among children. More commonly, a child will be unable or unwilling to express the insecurity caused by a newborn rival. Parents must read the subtle signs and clues. The most reliable symptom of the "I've-been-replaced" syndrome is a sudden return to infantile behavior. "If babyhood is where it's at, then I'll be a baby again." The child throws temper tantrums, wets the bed, sucks a thumb, holds tightly to Mama, and baby talks. A clear and present danger is being met in the best way known.

If a firstborn child seems to feel like a has-been, I would suggest following this procedure:

1. *Bring feelings out into the open and help the child verbalize them.* When a child is acting silly in front of adults, trying to make them laugh or notice, it is good to take him in your arms and say, "What's the matter, Joey? Do you need some attention today?" Gradually a child can be taught to use similar words when he feels excluded or rejected. "I need some attention, Dad. Will you play with me?" By verbalizing those feelings, the child also develops self-understanding.

2. *Don't let antisocial behavior succeed.* If the child cries when the babysitter arrives, leave anyway. Reveal little anger or other displeasure, remembering that the episode is motivated by a feeling that withdrawal of your love is threatened.

3. *Meet the child's needs in ways that grant status for being older.* Go to the park, making it clear that the baby is too little to go; talk "up" to him about the things he can do that the baby can't—use the bathroom instead of his pants, for example. Let the older child take care of the baby, to feel part of the family process. A telephone company produced a commercial that beautifully illustrates this strategy from a child's point of view. A child of four or five tells us how Mommy went to the hospital to have a new baby, and everyone was paying attention to the new kid. He says he was feeling left out—but then Mommy called him and explained that she was going to need his help to care for this helpless infant. That made everything better. The phone company is, of course, selling communication. In a case like this, communication is the idea.

It is not difficult to convey love to more than one child simultaneously, provided you put your mind (and heart) to it.

The first strategy, in summary, involves examining the emotional content of your home. Does it contribute to self-confidence or self-degradation? Does it meet the basic emotional needs, or does it leave family members unsatisfied and yearning? Does it reserve respect and admiration for the bright and beautiful child, or does it grant human worth to every person on earth? Does it reinforce the best in life or the worst? Someday, your grown child will look back in anger or appreciation, depending on the answers to these relevant questions.

Questions and Answers

What about good-natured teasing and joking within the family? Is it harmful to laugh about and kid each other?

The most healthy families can laugh together, and I certainly don't think our egos should be so fragile that we all have to walk on eggshells around each other. However, even innocent humor can be painful when one child is always the object of the jokes. When one youngster has an embarrassing feature, such as bed-wetting or thumb-sucking or stuttering or a striking physical flaw, other family members should be encouraged to tread softly on the exposed nerves. Particularly, one should not ridicule a child about size, whether a small boy or a large girl. There is nothing funny about that subject. This is the guiding principle: It is wise not to tease a child about the features he or she is also defending outside the home. And when the child asks that any joke should end, those wishes should be honored.

Must I praise my child all day for every little thing he does? Isn't it possible to create a spoiled brat by telling him his every move is wonderful?

Yes, inflationary praise is counterproductive. Junior quickly catches on to your verbal game, and your words lose their meaning. It is helpful to distinguish between the concepts of *flattery* versus *praise*. Flattery is unearned. It is what Grandma says when she comes for a visit: "Oh, look at my beautiful little girl! You're getting prettier each day. I'll bet you'll have to beat the boys off with a club when you get to be a teenager!" Or, "My, what a smart boy you are." Flattery occurs when you heap compliments upon a child for something he or she did not achieve.

Praise, on the other hand, reinforces positive, constructive behavior. It should be highly specific. "You've been a good boy" is unsatisfactory; "I like the way you kept your room straight today" is better. Parents should always watch for opportunities to offer genuine, deserved praise to their children, while avoiding empty flattery.

We live in "routine panic" in our home, as you described. I have three children under six, and I never get caught up with my work. How can I slow down when it takes every minute of the day (and night) to care for my children?

There may be a helpful answer in the way you spend your money. Most Americans maintain a "priority list" of things to purchase when enough money has been saved. They plan ahead to reupholster the sofa or carpet the dining-room floor or buy a newer car. However, it is my conviction that domestic help (a high-schooler, for instance) for the mother of small children should appear on that priority list too. Without it, she is sentenced to the same responsibility day in and day out, seven days a week. For several years she is unable to escape the unending burden of dirty diapers, runny noses, and unwashed dishes. It is my belief that she will do a more efficient job in those tasks and be a better mother if she can share the load with someone else occasionally. More explicitly, I feel she should get out of the house completely for one day a week, doing something for sheer enjoyment. This seems more important to the happiness of the home than buying new drapes or a power saw.

How can financially limited families afford housecleaning and baby-sitting services? Perhaps by using competent high school students instead of older adults. I would suggest placing a call to the counseling office of the nearest senior high school. Tell the counselor that you need a mature student to do some cleaning. Do not reveal that you are looking for a regular employee. When the referred girl arrives, try her out for a day to see how she handles responsibility. If she's very efficient, offer her a weekly job. If she is slow and flighty, thank her for coming and call for another student the following week. There are remarkable differences in maturity among high school girls, and you'll eventually find one who works like an adult. Be sure to check on the employee tax regulations that might pertain to a frequent helper.

I am very disappointed with the way my four-year-old is turning out. If the present trends continue, he will be a failure as an adult. Is it possible to "forecast" a child's future character and personality traits from this early age?

Rene Voeltzel said, "We must not look too soon in the child for the person he will later become." It is unfair and damaging to judge him too soon. Be patient and give your child time to mature. Work gently on the traits that concern you the most, but, by all means, allow the privilege to be a child. It will last for such a brief moment.

5

Defuse the Values Bomb

We have slipped behind the values lines to spy out enemies of confidence in our children. We have also checked to make sure we aren't giving aid and comfort to the enemies of our children. The time has come now to consider some strategic maneuvers to advance. This is a winnable war, though the values battlefield can be a frightening place for us as well as the kids.

In the early 1990s, the National Education Association estimated that 100,000 children were carrying guns to school daily. And 13 percent of gun-related incidents involved elementary and even kindergarten youngsters.[1] The nation is still staggered by the massacres in Littleton, Colorado, and Jonesboro, Arkansas. In urban and even some suburban schools, our kids are being approached by gang recruiters, often with threats if they refuse to get in the program. It takes a lot of confidence to "just say no" to some of the pressures encountered on today's elementary, middle, and secondary school campuses. In class, a teacher may advocate the "multicultural" children's book, *Daddy's Roommate* by Michael Wilhoite, or some similar work that teaches the acceptability of an active homosexual lifestyle. At a school dance, parent chaperones or school administrators may be passing out latex condoms.

Toto, I don't think we're in Kansas anymore.

Does that mean the battle has been lost during the twenty-five years this book has been in print? Absolutely not. It does give those of you who are parenting today's toddlers even more motivation than your parents had to arm your son and daughter with an awareness of the values war and a strong sense of self-worth. In this chapter we present strategies to help your children withstand the pressures that confront them.

Strategy 2: Reserve Adolescence for the Adolescents

In recent decades, toy manufacturers and other interests have successfully changed the nature of children's play. Instead of three- and four-year-old boys and girls playing with stuffed animals, balls, cars, trucks, model horses, and other traditional memorabilia of childhood, they learn to fantasize about life as an adolescent. The most influential force behind this trend has been the Barbie doll marketers. I am unalterably opposed to the entire concept! There is in the late 1990s some pressure to tone down the overt sexuality of these figures and make them a little less idealized. On the other hand, the

African-American Barbie has been redesigned to be even more of an ideal for black youngsters, and there are now dolls on the ethnic and international market shelves with Native American, Arab, Asian, and Spanish racial characteristics. Rather than being a wholesome reaching out to minorities, this marketing ploy makes matters worse. Now every Spanish kid is even more strongly pulled toward the "adolescence-means-beauty-and-materialism" idol. This is not a positive role model for anyone. Kuwait drew laughter when the nation banned Barbie dolls from its toy market. I can appreciate the Kuwait leaders' motivation completely.

However the plastic dyes are tweaked, the general ideas remain in place. There could be no better method for teaching the worship of beauty and materialism than with this plastic role model and all her fashions and possessions. If we intentionally sought to drill our babies on the necessity of growing up rich and gorgeous, we could do no better. Even if future models go through bust reduction, we are not likely to see an unglamorous or imperfect Barbie doll. Her hair is thick and gleaming—loaded with "body," whatever in the world that is. Her airbrushed skin is without blemish, except for a little statement on her bottom that she was "Made in Japan." She never gets pimples or blackheads. Not only is Barbie one of the beautiful people but so are all her buddies. Her swinging boyfriend, Ken, is an adolescent composite of Kurt Russell and Young Indiana Jones. These idealized models load an emotional time bomb set to explode the moment a real live thirteen-year-old takes her first long look in the mirror. No doubt about it—Barbie she ain't.

Yet it is not the physical perfection of these Barbie dolls (and their many competitors) that concerns me most. Of greater harm are the teenage games they inspire. Ken and Barbie go on dates, learn to dance, drive sports cars, get suntans, take camping trips, exchange marriage vows, and have babies (hopefully in that order). The entire adolescent culture, with its emphasis on sexual awareness, is illustrated to tiny little girls who ought to be thinking about more childish things. This places our children on an unnatural timetable likely to reach the peak of sexual interest several years before it is due—with all the obvious implications for their social and emotional health.

We not only teach our small children about adolescent values through their toys, but we hit 'em with an effective one-two punch! Television, particularly the Saturday morning variety, is loaded with teenage idealization. It is pointless to mention the names and plotlines of cartoons, after-school programming, and prime-time sitcoms feeding on the teen market and their younger siblings. These change every time network advertisers make a new study of what teens are spending their billions of discretionary dollars to buy. It isn't that program merchandisers have forgotten that smaller faces are in the line of fire. Fortunes are waiting to be made in shaping desires for the name-brand clothing and cosmetics as soon as possible. Since the U.S. Congress passed the Children's Television Act of 1990, government and social science have been desperately trying to tone down the product promotion as well as the sex and violence in children's TV. Whatever ratings system and regulations are passed will do minimal good. The most "innocent" of programs design perfect teenage models for the preteen set, who respond with appropriate crushes and fan mail. All this accounts, in part, for the trend toward younger dating and sexual awareness.

Much the same can be said about video games. One recent Japanese import features a cartoon heroine about nineteen or twenty years of age who appears to have been poured into her black leather jumpsuit with the neckline that goes down to somewhere around the belly button. This young ideal is aimed at preadolescent boys, the number one user of such toys being eight- to twelve-year-olds. What values message is this game player soaking up as he helps this sexual dynamo blast away the baddies with her extensive arsenal of weapons? Reports one recent look at this industry: "The video-game industry is being propelled forward by a technological imperative that is reshaping most forms of entertainment. America's telemedia giants . . . are spending billions to turn today's passive television broadcast system into a two-way, interactive information highway capable of delivering not just movies, sitcoms and news on demand, but the world's greatest video games as well."[2] The industry has sought to involve as many adults as possible, but the video-game market has not drastically changed over the years. Everyone admits that the number one target is the preadolescent boy.

We cannot isolate our small children from the world as it is, but we don't have to cooperate in turning our babies into teenyboppers.

Parents should also keep a wary eye on the values at the fingertips of the web surfer. My greatest concern about the internet is that there are now 160,000 pornographic sites available at the click of the keyboard. Many of them offer free "teasers" to pull viewers—including children—into the most horrible material. Indeed, the categories are often intended to attract children.

"Toys," for example, can bring up "sex toys"; "horses" can introduce bestiality. A boy or girl who regularly uses the internet *will* eventually stumble into explicit images. Programs are available to lock sexually explicit websites, but with thousands of new sites added daily, these programs are not fail-safe. Nor do they deal with one of the most insidious values bases, the online marketplace where tantalizing goodies of every description are described by "SPAM" junk email messages. The world is yours with one click of a mouse (and a credit card number). The pre-credit card set may not be able to buy, but little noses are pressed against the store window. Mom and Dad need to spend some time with children who are into cyberspace. If you can't work the internet, don't worry; your seven-year-old will explain it. But then you two need to talk about the meaning of some of the things found there.[3]

I believe it is desirable to postpone the adolescent experience until it is summoned by the happy hormones. Therefore, I strongly recommend that parents screen the internet, video games, television, and other media influences to which their children are exposed, keeping activities appropriate for each age. And *anything* that tells your child to be beautiful and rich should be viewed with suspicion. We cannot isolate our small children from the world as it is, but we don't have to cooperate in turning our babies into teenyboppers.

Questions and Answers

Do you think children between five and ten should be allowed to listen to rock music on the radio?

Not if it can be prevented gracefully. Here again, rock, rap, and country music express an adolescent-and-beyond culture. Even the most innocuous songs teens listen to deal with dating, broken hearts, drug use, and a preoccupation with sexuality. This is just what you don't want your seven-year-old thinking about. Instead, his world of excitement should consist of adventure books and family activities—camping, fishing, sporting events, and games. In the first edition of this book I suggested Disney-type television productions. Now I would qualify that to include the type of adventure-oriented stories that were produced when Walt Disney was alive. That may mean relying on a stock of carefully selected purchased and rented videos in place of the cable or satellite feed, even if it does have 150 stations from which to choose.

Speaking of the Disney Corporation and its subsidiaries, their recent creations would make its legendary founder turn in his grave. The company that gave us *Winnie the Pooh* and *Snow White* now peddles extremely objectionable films and television programs that can hardly be termed "family friendly." Under its Miramax film subsidiary, Disney has offered such movies as *Kids*, *Trainspotting*, and *Clerks*. *Kids* opens with a boy nicknamed "the virgin surgeon" deflowering a fourteen-year-old girl, and in the words of one *Newsweek* writer, "follows a number of barely-pubescent-looking boys and girls around New York City as they smoke pot, bait gays, beat a black man and engage in graphic sex." Disney's *Trainspotting* puts an attractive Hollywood spin on heroin addiction while *Clerks* (originally rated NC-17) records the explicit sexual dialogue and fantasies of a convenience store employee. Disney's *Scream* (Dimension Films/$100 million-plus at the box office) opens with a teenage girl being stalked, stabbed, gutted, and hung from a tree in her own backyard. Any company that produces this kind of wicked material is not "family friendly" and isn't worthy of parental support. Why does it surprise us that children are becoming more violent and promiscuous in today's world?

What is your view of TV generally? Should parents attempt to regulate what their children watch?

I have some serious concerns about television's impact on our society, and particularly on our younger generation. According to Dr. Gerald Looney, University of Arizona, by the time the average preschool child reaches fourteen years of age he will have witnessed eighteen thousand murders on TV and countless hours of related violence, nonsense, and unadulterated drivel. As *U.S. News* reports, "Between the ages of 6 and 18, American children on average watch 15,000 hours of television. That's 2,000 hours more than time spent in school."[4]

Congress and the Federal Communications Commission have authorized ratings to give parents some clues about what is coming, but these are of limited help in discerning values and worldview. And other aspects of television demand its regulation and control. For one thing, it is an enemy of communication within the family. How can we talk to each other when a million-dollar production in living color is beckoning our attention? I am also concerned about the current fashion whereby each program director is compelled to push the envelope farther and farther into profanity, bad taste, indecency, and counter-Judeo-Christian values. Consider the subject matter of abortion, divorce, extramarital relationships, rape, prostitution, and the acceptability of an active, open homosexual lifestyle. If this is "social relevance," I am sick unto death of the messages I have been fed.

Today's sitcoms often include a homosexual character, who is used by the writers to break down opposition to the gay lifestyle. Television has an awesome power to fulfill its own prophecies. As producers try to be "on the edge" of modern life, they often lead society over the edge.

While some observers hail the educational power of TV, others fear its negative influence. Daniel R. Anderson, a University of Massachusetts psychology professor and coauthor of a major study of TV's impact on children's education, believes that television is teaching children to be violent in order to be respected.

Neil Postman, media critic and author of the book *Amusing Ourselves to Death,* discounts the educational benefit even of educational programs. Real-life teachers can't compete. "*Sesame Street* makes children like school, only if school is like *Sesame Street.*" Postman and other critics add that television "gives away the secrets of adulthood," and gives children a rather superficial view of adult life. "What I see happening is a blurring of childhood and adulthood," Postman has written of the effect of television.[5]

I'm also concerned about cartoons that indulge in considerable violence, feature adult activities, and have an occult or New Age flavor. The action often revolves around superstition, sorcery, and magic. These cartoons seem to be teaching subtle spiritual (rather, false-spiritual) messages.

Author Marie Winn Anderson believes that TV, of any kind, destroys family relationships. "Parents use television in daily child rearing as a problem solver," she says. "When young children start to fight, they'll say, 'Gee, *Sesame Street* is on.' But they haven't solved the problem. Before television, parents had to be firmer."[6]

She's right. In some ways, TV gives parents an easy out. They don't have to deal with their children as much. It's certainly tempting to let the tube babysit the kids, but after a while the TV becomes the parent, and you're the stranger. And, as we've seen, in terms of values, TV makes a lousy parent.

As Anderson says, "Unsupervised TV is like letting your children play out on the street at any hour of the day or night with whomever they come across."[7]

Is that really possible, to go without TV? Won't that stunt my kids' creativity?

In 1974, Marie Winn organized the Denver No-TV experiment. A writer and mother, Winn asked a columnist for the *Denver Post* to invite parents to participate in the month-long, no-TV experiment, keeping a diary of results. Fifteen families shared their diaries with Winn. All experienced a withdrawal period, followed by a euphoria with better communication between children and adults, a more peaceful atmosphere, greater closeness as a family, and more leisurely meals.[8]

So, it is *possible* to do without TV. However, I don't think it is *necessary* to go without TV entirely. Television still has great potential to put on good programs, and every so often a series comes along that tries to present and support good family values. I would not, therefore, recommend smashing the TV set in despair. We must learn to control it, instead of becoming its slave.

> *It's certainly tempting to let the tube babysit the kids, but after a while the TV becomes the parent, and you're the stranger.*

When our children were growing up, Shirley and I allowed one hour of cartoons on Saturday morning and a half-hour program each afternoon, selected from an approved list. We kept the policy flexible in the case of special programs of interest. In this way, we could take advantage of the benefits of television without letting it dominate our lives.

And, as noted above, many good programs are available on children's videos. Obviously, many of the programs offered for sale or rental have the same problems as TV shows. But there are many wholesome programs—and there is a substantial amount of Christian video programming. We have tried to add to it at Focus on the Family with such productions as *Odyssey, Last Chance Detectives*, and other video and audio offerings. They are geared for eight- to twelve-year-olds and try to express Christian values in an entertaining, dramatic form. And there are many teaching, music, and Bible story tapes from which to choose.

One word of caution, however. Even good TV or video becomes bad when there's too much of it. If your child spends time in front of the tube when he should be doing homework or chores, talking with you, or playing outside, that's a problem. You shouldn't let any media—even *McGee and Me*—do your parenting for you.

Strategy 3: Teach Your Child a "No-Knock" Policy

One of the most obvious characteristics of a person who feels inferior is that he talks about deficiencies to anyone who will listen. An obese person feels compelled to apologize to companions for ordering a hot fudge sundae. He echoes what he imagines they are thinking: "I'm already fat enough without eating this," he says, scooping up the cherry and syrup with his spoon. Likewise, a woman who thinks she's dumb will admit freely, "I am really bad at math; I can hardly add two and two." This kind of self-denigration is not as uncommon as one might think. Listen to yourself over time. You might be surprised by how often you emphasize your faults to your friends.

While there is no virtue in becoming an image-conscious phony, trying to be something you are not, it is also a mistake to go to the other extreme. While you are babbling about all of your ridiculous inadequacies, the listener is formulating an impression of you. That person will later "see" you and treat you according to the evidence you've provided. After all, you're the expert on that subject. Further, having put your feelings into words, they become solidified as fact in your own mind.

Therefore, we should teach a "no-knock" policy to our children. They should learn that constant self-criticism can become a bad habit, and it accomplishes nothing. There is a big difference between accepting blame when it is valid and in simply chattering about one's inferiority.

Questions and Answers

What do children most often dislike about themselves?

For a book by E. A. Douvan, *Adolescent Girls*, nearly two thousand girls from eleven to eighteen years of age were asked, "What would you most like to change about yourself if you could ... your looks, your personality, or your life!" Fifty-nine percent mentioned some aspect of their physical appearance. Only 4 percent desired greater ability. The most common personal dissatisfaction for both boys and girls concerns facial defects, primarily skin problems. In a later study by H. V. Cobb, children in grades four and older were asked to complete the sentence, "I wish I were . . ." The majority of the boys answered "taller" and the girls answered "smaller." Certainly there is a great volume of scientific evidence to document children's preoccupation and dissatisfaction with their own physical characteristics.

My child is often ridiculed and hurt by the other children on our block, and I don't know how to handle the situation. He gets very depressed and comes home crying frequently. How should I respond when this happens?

When your child has been rejected in this manner, he is badly in need of a friend—and you are elected. Let him talk. Don't try to tell him that it doesn't hurt or that it's silly to be so sensitive. Ask him if he knows what it is that his "friends" don't like. He may be causing their reaction by dominance, selfishness, or dishonesty. Be understanding and sympathetic without weeping in mutual despair. As soon as appropriate, involve yourself with him in a game or some other activity he will enjoy. Finally, set about resolving the underlying cause.

I would suggest that you ask your child to invite one of his school friends to go to the zoo on Saturday, or offer some other attractive "bait." They might spend the night at your house. Genuine friendship often grows from such beginnings. Even the hostile children on the block may be more kind when only one of them is invited at a time. Not only can you help your child make friends in this way, but you can observe the social mistakes he is making to drive them away. The information you gain can later be used to help him improve his relationships with others.

My ten-year-old daughter hates to have her hair braided because her friends don't wear theirs that way. Am I wrong to make her please me by wearing her hair the way I want it?

Yes, particularly if it makes your daughter feel unnecessarily different and foolish with her friends. Social pressure on the nonconformist is severe, and you should not place your daughter in this uncomfortable position. Closeness between generations comes from the child's knowledge that parents understand and appreciate feelings. Your inflexibility on this point reveals a lack of empathy and may bring later resentment.

Strategy 4: Help Your Child Compensate

Now let's get down to the nitty-gritty. Some children have much greater handicaps than others and are almost certainly destined for emotional trouble during adolescence. Their anxious parents can see it coming like a gathering storm, even prior to the school years. Perhaps a child has an unattractive appearance or a severe learning problem. For whatever reason, everybody can see that he or she is going to get clobbered by life. What can parents do to prepare this child to confront a most unsympathetic world?

Compensation is your child's best weapon against inferiority. This means that the individual counterbalances weaknesses by capitalizing on strengths. There are no simple "cures" to eliminate the struggle, short of changing the values of an entire society. Some books on self-esteem assert that parental love, if vigorously expressed every day, is all that a child needs to develop self-confidence. I wish that were true, but in fact, a child's self-view is a product of two important influences: the quality of home life and social experiences outside the family. The first of these forces is much easier to control than the second. There is no emotional armor that will make your child impervious to rejection and ridicule in social contacts. It always hurts to be laughed at, snubbed, ignored, or attacked by others. But I would remind you at this point that the human personality grows through mild adversity, provided it is not crushed in the process. Contrary to what you might believe, the ideal environment for your child is not one devoid of problems and trials. I would not, even if I could, have swept aside every hurdle from the paths of my children, leaving them to glide along in mirth through childhood. They deserve the right to face problems and profit from the confrontation.

My childhood was remarkably happy and carefree. I was loved beyond any doubt, and my academic performance was never a cause for discomfort. In fact, I have enjoyed happiness and fulfillment, with the exception of two painful years. Those stressful days occurred during my seventh and eighth grade experience, through ages thirteen and fourteen. During this period, I found myself in a social crossfire, giving rise to the same intense feelings of inferiority and self-doubt I have described herein. As strange as it seems, however, these two years contributed more positive features to my adult personality than any other span of which I am aware. My empathy for others, my desire to succeed in life, my motivation in graduate school, my understanding of inferiority, and my communication with teenagers are primarily the product of an agitated adolescence. Who would have thought anything useful would have come from those twenty-four months? Yet the discomfort proved to be a valuable instructor in this instance.

Though it is hard to accept at the time, your child also needs the minor setbacks and disappointments that come along. If early experiences are without trial, then how will one learn to cope with problems and frustration? A tree planted in a rain forest is never forced to extend its roots downward in search of water. Consequently it remains poorly anchored and can be toppled by a moderate windstorm. By contrast, a mesquite tree planted in a dry desert is threatened by its hostile environment. It can only survive by sending its roots more than thirty feet deep into the earth, seeking cool water. But through its adaptation to the arid land, something else happens. The well-rooted tree becomes strong and steady against all assailants. This illustration applies to our children. Those who have learned to conquer their problems are more secure than those who have never faced them. Our task as parents, then, is not to eliminate every challenge for our children; it is to serve as a confident ally on their behalf, encouraging when they are distressed, intervening when the threats are overwhelming, and above all, giving them the tools with which to overcome the obstacles.

One of those vital tools involves compensation. It is our job as parents to help our children find those strengths and learn to exploit them for all the self-satisfaction they will yield. And this brings us to a very important concept to be grasped: Inferiority can either crush and paralyze an individual, or it can provide tremendous emotional energy to power every kind of success and achievement. Where do you suppose the former world's champion chess player, Bobby Fischer, got the drive and ambition to read chess, play chess, think chess, and dream chess twenty-four hours a day? "It was some people thinking maybe I wasn't as good as they were when I was a kid," Fischer said.

Where do you think the great writer Thomas Wolfe derived the energy and stamina to sit at a typewriter for eighteen or twenty hours a day, months at a time? What pushes a distance runner to plod along for ten miles in the lonely sand before the sun rises each morning? What inner need propels a student into the rigors of medical school, pushing to the limits of endurance through years of mental discipline? The power behind these and other kinds of success almost invariably springs from the need for self-worth, the need to prove something about one's adequacy, the need to compensate.

Will your child collapse under the weight of inferiority or use it to supercharge personal initiative and drive? Will he or she "hide" or "seek"? The answer probably will depend on the availability of compensatory skills. It is your job as a parent to help find them. Perhaps your child can establish a niche in music—many children do. Maybe the child can develop artistic talent or learn to write or cultivate mechanical skills or build model airplanes or raise rabbits for fun and profit. Regardless of the choice, the key is to start down that road early. There is nothing more risky than to send a teenager into the storms of adolescence with no skills, no unique knowledge, no means of compensating. When this occurs, his or her ego is stark naked. He cannot say, "I may not be the most popular student in school, but I am the best trumpet player in the band!" His only source of self-esteem comes from the acceptance of other students—and their love is notoriously fickle.

Is compensation an alternative only for those children who are particularly gifted in an area? Certainly not. There is something emotionally satisfying for nearly everyone, if the person can find it. I saw this process in operation even among those of very meager ability when I was working at Pacific State Hospital for the Mentally Retarded in Pomona, California. Every afternoon, for example, I heard a blaring trombone concert coming from a nearby hillside, something vaguely recognizable as John Philip Sousa marches. I had no idea who was responsible for the serenades. Then one day as I walked across the grounds of the hospital, a patient about seventeen years old ran up to me and said: "Hi. My name is James Walter Jackson (not his actual name). I'm the fellow who plays the trombone. Now I need your help to get a message through to Santa Claus, because I've gotta have a new trombone. The one I have is all beat up, and I want a brand new, silver Olds, with purple velvet lining in the case. Will you tell him that for me?"

There is nothing more risky than to send a teenager into the storms of adolescence with no skills, no unique knowledge, no means of compensating. When this occurs, his or her ego is stark naked.

I was a bit taken aback, but I volunteered to do what I could. That afternoon as I discussed James Walter Jackson with another staff member, he gave me a little background on the message to Santa. The year before, this patient had told several people that he would like Santa Claus to bring him a trombone. One of the hospital workers had an old instrument in the garage that had about seen its day, so on Christmas morning it was donated to James Walter Jackson with credit given to Santa.

James was delighted, of course, but he was a bit disappointed by all those bumps and dings. He figured he hadn't been specific enough in his prior message to Santa, so he would do better next time. He launched a year-long campaign designed to let the North Pole know exactly what he had in mind. He stopped everyone he met on the street and told them precisely what to tell Santa.

Shortly after that, I saw James Walter Jackson for the last time. I was driving out of the hospital grounds when I noticed this amicable patient in the rearview mirror. He was running down the road behind my car, waving for me to stop. I pulled to the curb and let him catch up with me. He put his head in the window and said, panting, "Don't forget to tell him that I want the long-lasting kind!" I hope someone bought James Walter Jackson what he wanted so badly. His ability to compensate depended on it.

Without question, the richest harvest of compensation in the adolescent world can be found in athletics. This has long been true for boys, and it has recently become applicable for girls as well. In a study of ten representative northern Illinois high schools by James S. Coleman, he asked students to indicate the values that were of greatest importance to them. For girls, beauty outranked every other factor. For boys, athletic ability came in first place, which is just another dimension of physical factors. Size, strength, coordination, and speed can be separated from physical features themselves. As might be expected, educational achievement ranked very low on both boys' and girls' hierarchy of values.

Because of the status athletes have in today's high schools, I believe this avenue of compensation should be explored by the parents of "high-risk" boys, in particular. A child who is reasonably coordinated can be taught to play basketball, football, tennis, or golf. The key to athletic excellence is to start early. We do not hesitate to provide piano lessons to eight-year-olds; why should we not give basketball training at the same age?

This raises a point of controversy. Many parents feel they do not have the right to introduce a new activity to their child. They sit back in the hopes that he will make it for himself. However, most children are remarkably undisciplined. It is always difficult to learn a new skill—particularly during the initial stages. There is no fun to be derived from total failure, which is the typical feeling in the beginning. Thus, the child never learns those important skills that will be so badly needed later on. I recommend that you, the parents, make a careful assessment of areas of strength, then select a skill in which the greatest possibilities for success lie. Once this selection is made, see the child through the first stage. Reward, push, threaten, beg, bribe if necessary, but make the child learn it. If you discover later that you've made a mistake, back up and start over on something else. But don't let inertia keep you from teaching something emotionally useful to your offspring! Does this form of coercion impinge upon the freedom of the child to choose? Perhaps, but so does making the child learn to eat properly, keep clean, and go to bed at a reasonable hour. It is, as they say, in the child's best interest.

My own dad decided when I was eight years old that he was going to teach me to play tennis. I was not at all enthusiastic about this offer. My dad didn't mess around when he decided to teach me something. I knew it meant drill and sweat and blisters. I would rather have played cowboys with my friends in the neighborhood. But my dad wanted me to play tennis, and I respected him too much to turn him down. So we spent several agonizing Saturdays on the court. He would hit me a ball, and I'd whack it over the fence and then have to go get it. I couldn't have been less motivated, but I tried to act involved. "You think I'm getting it, Dad?" I asked as another ball flew straight up.

About a month later, however, things began to click. I started to feel good when I hit the ball correctly. One afternoon a fellow my age came up and asked if I'd play him a game. Well, I'd never thought about it, but I didn't see why not. So we played a set of tennis—and I beat him—and I liked that. I slowly began to realize what this game had to offer me. A spark of enthusiasm turned into a source of self-confidence. If asked to write, "Who am I?" during the trials of adolescence, I would have begun, "I am the number-one tennis player in the high school." If my dad had not planted his thumb in my back, urging me to try something new, I'd have never known what I missed. I am thankful that he helped me compensate. Have you done as much for your child?

Questions and Answers

My fifteen-year-old is a nature-lover through and through. His room is filled with caged snakes, wasps' nests, plants, and insects. Even the garage is occupied by various animals he has caught and tamed. I hate all this stinky stuff and want him to get interested in something else. What should I do?

If he keeps his zoo clean and well managed, then you should let him follow his interests. Just remember that at fifteen, "bugs" beat "drugs" as a hobby.

My son is an outstanding gymnast. His high school coach says he has more natural ability than anyone he's ever seen. Yet when he is being judged in a competitive meet he does terribly! Why does he fail during the most important moments?

If your son thinks of himself as a failure, his performance will probably match his low self-image when the chips are down. In the same way, there are many excellent golfers in the PGA tour who make a satisfactory living in tournament play, but they never win. They consistently place second, third, sixth, or tenth. Whenever it looks like they might come in first, they "choke" at the last minute and let someone else win. It is not that they want to fail; rather, they don't "see" themselves as winners. Their performance merely reflects this image.

I talked with a concert pianist of outstanding talent who has resolved never to play in public again. She knows she is blessed with remarkable ability but believes she is a loser in every other regard. Consequently, when she plays the piano on stage, her mistakes make her sound like a beginner. Every time this mortifying experience has occurred she has become more convinced of her own unworthiness in *every* area. She has now withdrawn into the secluded, quiet, talentless world of the have-nots.

There is no question about it: A lack of self-confidence can completely immobilize a talented person, simply through the threat of failure.

Is this true of mental ability too? My twelve-year-old was asked to recite a poem at a school function the other day, and he went completely blank in front of the crowd. I know he knew the poem perfectly because he had said it dozens of times at home. He's a bright child, but he's had this trouble before. Why does his mind "turn off" when he's under pressure?

It will be helpful to understand an important characteristic of intellectual functioning. Your son's self-confidence, or the lack of it, actually affects the way his brain operates. All of us have experienced the frustration of mental "blocking," which you described. This occurs when a name or fact or idea just won't surface to the conscious mind, even though we know it is recorded in the memory. Or suppose we are about to speak to an antagonistic group, and our mind suddenly goes blank. This kind of blocking usually occurs when social pressure is great and self-confidence is low. Why? Because emotions affect the efficiency of the human brain. Unlike a computer, our mental apparatus only functions properly when a delicate biochemical balance exists between the neural cells. This substance makes it possible for a cell to "fire" its electrochemical charge across the gap (synapse) to another cell. It is now known that a sudden emotional reaction can instantly change the nature of that biochemistry, blocking the impulse. This blockage prevents the electrical charge from being relayed, and the thought is never generated. This mechanism has profound implications for human behavior. A child who feels inferior and intellectually inadequate often does not even make use of available mental power. Lack of confidence disrupts mental processing, and the two go around and around in an endless cycle of defeat. This is obviously what happened when your son "forgot" the poem.

What can I do to help him?

Actually, it is not unusual for a twelve-year-old to "choke" in front of a crowd. I once stood before three hundred fellow teenagers with my words stuck in my throat and my mind totally out to lunch. It was a painful experience, but time gradually erased its impact. As your child matures, he will probably overcome the problem, if he can experience a few successes to build his confidence. Anything that raises self-esteem will reduce the frequency of mental blocking for children and adults alike.

Strategy 5: Help Your Child Compete

A parent who strongly opposes the emphasis society places on beauty and brains must resolve a difficult philosophical question. While he recognizes the injustice of this value system, his child is forced to compete in a world that worships those attributes. Should he help his youngster become as attractive as possible? Should he encourage his "average" child to excel in school? Or would he be wise to de-emphasize those values at home, hoping the child will learn to live with the handicaps?

Since the world is our ballpark, we cannot completely ignore the rules of the game. But . . . we can take comfort in knowing that the game itself is not that important.

There are no "scientific" answers to those questions. I can only give you my considered opinion. Despite the injustice of this system, my child will not be the one to change it. I am obligated to help him compete in his world as best he can. If his ears protrude, I will have them flattened. If his teeth are crooked, I will see that they are straightened. If he flounders academically, I will seek tutorial assistance to pull him out. He and I are allies in the fight for survival, and I will not turn a deaf ear to his needs.

Rick Barry, a former basketball star with the Golden State Warriors, as a child was humiliated and self-conscious about his teeth. As he described in the book, *Confessions of a Basketball Gypsy*:

> When my second teeth came in, they came in crooked and two of them were missing in front. Maybe my folks could not afford to have them fixed, or maybe having teeth fixed was not then what it is now. I remember talking to Dad about putting in false teeth in front and wearing braces, which might cut my gums when I exerted myself playing ball. Anyway, I did not have my teeth fixed until I was in college. I was very sensitive about my teeth. I was ashamed to look at myself in the mirror. I used to keep my mouth shut and I'd never smile. I used to keep my hand over my mouth, which muffled my voice and made it hard for people to understand me. I developed this habit of keeping my hand over my mouth, just sort of always resting on my chin, and I couldn't shake it for years afterward.[9]

What similar discomfort is your child experiencing in silence today? Isn't it our obligation, within the limits of financial resources, to eradicate the flaws that generate the greatest sensitivity? I believe it is, and the job should be done early. Dr. Edward Podolsky, assistant supervisory psychiatrist, Kings County Hospital, New York City, believes physical deformities should be corrected before the child enters first grade and peers begin to damage personal esteem.

But we parents must walk a tightrope at this point. While I am helping my child to compete in the world as it is, I must also teach him that its values are temporal and unworthy. Explaining the two contradictory sides of that coin requires considerable skill and tact. How can I urge my daughter to fix her hair neatly and then tell her, "Beauty doesn't matter"? The key is to begin very early to instruct the child on the *true* values of life: love for others, kindness, integrity, trustworthiness, truthfulness, and devotion to God. Physical attractiveness is then described as part of a social game we must play. Since the world is our ballpark, we cannot completely ignore the rules of the game. But whether we hit a home run or strike out, we can take comfort in knowing that the game itself is not that important. Herein lies an anchor that can hold a child steady.

Questions and Answers

My thirteen-year-old daughter is still built like a boy, but she is insisting that her mother buy her a bra. Believe me, she has no need for it, and the only reason she wants to wear one is because most of her friends do. Should I give in?

Your straight and narrow daughter needs a bra to be like her friends, to compete, to avoid ridicule, and to feel like a woman. Those are excellent reasons. Your wife should meet this request by tomorrow morning, if not sooner.

My older child is a great student and earns straight A's year after year. Her younger sister, now in the sixth grade, is completely bored with school and won't even try. The frustrating thing is

*that the younger girl is probably brighter than her older sister.
Why would she refuse to apply her ability like this?*

There could be many reasons for her academic disinterest, but let me suggest the most probable explanation. Children will often refuse to compete when they think they are likely to place second instead of first. Therefore, a younger child may diligently avoid challenging an older sibling in her area of greatest strength. If son number one is a great athlete, then son number two may be more interested in collecting butterflies. If daughter number one is a disciplined pianist, then daughter number two may be a boy-crazy goof-off.

This rule does not always hold, of course, depending on the child's fear of failure and the way she estimates her chances of successful competition. If her confidence is high, she may blatantly wade into the territory owned by big sister, determined to do even better. However, the more typical response is to seek new areas of compensation that are not yet dominated by a family superstar.

If this explanation fits the behavior of your younger daughter, then it would be wise to accept something less than perfection from her school performance. Every child need not fit the same mold—nor can we force them to do so.

What happens when a child is so different from the group that he cannot compete, no matter how hard he tries?

That dead-end street is most often responsible for attempts at self-destruction. I am reminded of a sad little girl named Lily, an eighth-grader who was referred to me for psychological counseling. She opened the door to my office and stood with eyes cast down. Underneath several layers of powder and makeup, her face was completely aglow with infected acne.

Lily had done her best to bury the inflammation, but she had not been successful. She weighed about eighty-five pounds and was a physical wreck from head to toe. She sat down without raising her eyes to mine, lacking the confidence to face me. I didn't need to ask what was troubling her. Life had dealt her a devastating blow, and she was bitter, angry, broken, and deeply hurt. The teenager who reaches this point of despair can see no tomorrow. There is no hope. She can't think of anything else. The adolescent feels repulsive and disgusting and would like to crawl into a hole, but there is no place to hide. Running away won't help, nor will crying change anything. Too often suicide seems the best way out.

Lily gave me little time to work. The following morning she staggered into the school office and announced that she had ingested everything in the family medicine cabinet. We labored feverishly to retrieve the medication and finally succeeded on the way to the hospital. Lily survived physically, but her self-esteem and confidence had died years earlier. The scars on her sad face symbolized the wounds on her adolescent heart.

Suicide is occurring more frequently among American teenagers. An estimated 10,000 U.S. teens kill themselves each year according to Steven D. Padgitt, PhD, of the Turn On to Teens organization of Fresno, California. The adolescent suicide rate nearly tripled between 1950 and 1980[10] and increased another 10 percent by 1990. Suicide is the third leading cause of death for teenagers. A 1996 survey of 10,904 high school students sponsored by the Centers for Disease Control found that 18.3 percent of teenage boys and 30.4 percent of teenage girls had thought seriously about killing themselves.

Another significant statistic is that the suicide rate rises with the population rate. That is, when there are more teen-agers in society scrambling for attention and success and scholarships, a higher percentage of them commit suicide. As the *Journal of the American Medical Association* suggests, with more youngsters comes greater competition for limited resources, be they environmental (such as mental health services and jobs) or emotional (such as parental or teacher attention and academic honors).[11]

Other studies of suicide victims concur: Suicide victims find it hard to compete in an increasingly competitive ado-lescent society. The fact is, they are not just competing for honors. They are competing for their very identity. Their society assures them that losers are worth nothing. Why not end the agony of nothingness by taking your own life? If I am nothing, they figure, I have nothing to lose.

Parents must wisely play both ends of this game. They must help their children compete socially, academically, athletically, and in other ways, while assuring their children that they have immense worth whether they win or lose in society's struggles.

6

Parent Positively

A parent has little control over many areas of life. But fortunately, you have the greatest influence where it really matters; positive parenting makes all the difference when your child hits life's challenges. What are the positive-parenting strategies? The first is discipline. Parents have a divine mandate to shape and direct their children. True, youngsters can be exasperating, rebellious, and willful, so that wise discipline seems the impossible challenge. But the reality of discipline is that it is worth all the trouble to mold clay of infinite and eternal value.

Further, positive parenting means close involvement in what goes into the mind of that valuable lump of clay. It doesn't take an education degree to take charge of the educational process. The most important contribution a parent can make is to recognize the signs of defeat and befuddlement. You are your child's most important ally in smoothing out the bumps along learning's highway. Of course behind all the discipline and education is the big picture—you are trying to work yourselves out of the Mom-and-Dad job. From infancy on, parenting should move a dependent child toward independent and responsible adulthood.

The final aspect of positive parenting to be discussed in this chapter is character development. The strategy here is to encourage the growth of a kind, others-centered human being, who builds up rather than tears down the confidence of others.

Strategy 6: Discipline without Damaging Self-Worth

We now deal with the very important question of discipline and self-esteem. Does punishment, particularly spanking, break the spirit of the child? The answer to this question depends entirely on the manner and intent of the parents. The issue is not, "to spank or not to spank"; it is "how, in what way, and for what?" While this subject was discussed in my book, *Dare to Discipline*,[1] it needs to be reexamined here, specifically in relation to the child's self-concept.

A spanking is a very worthwhile tool when used properly, and I strongly urge its periodic application to the bottoms of America's youngest generation. However, like any tool, it can be applied correctly or incorrectly. Belief in corporal punishment is certainly no excuse for taking out your frustrations and anxieties on little Johnny. It won't justify cracking him behind the ear for his mistakes, accidents, and childish irresponsibility. It offers no license to punish him in front of others or treat him with general disrespect. I counseled one unfortunate teenager whose brutal father had beaten her throughout childhood. On one occasion, after she had accidentally wet her bed during the night, he wrapped her head in the urine-soaked sheet and pushed her into the toilet, upside down. Her self-concept will never recover from the nightmares he inflicted on her tender mind. No one can doubt that this kind of fierce, hostile, undeserved, and whimsical punishment can be devastating to a youngster, particularly one who feels unloved at home. There are, then, psychological dangers to be avoided.

Discipline and Belonging

On the other hand, another highly effective way to damage confidence is to avoid disciplinary control altogether. When a child knows he has done wrong, especially when selfish or offensive to others, he expects his parents to respond appropriately. After all, they are the symbols of justice, law, and order, which every child loves. Their refusal to accept the challenge is viewed with disrespect. They may seem unworthy of allegiance. More important, why would they let him do such things if they really loved him? In the Bible, the Book of Hebrews states this bit of wisdom explicitly: "If you are left without discipline, in which all have participated, then you are illegitimate children and not sons" (Hebrews 12:8 RSV).

How true this is! An undisciplined child feels like he does not belong in the family, despite the "love" of parents. Stanley Coopersmith, associate professor of psychology at the University of California, studied 1,738 normal middle-class boys and their families, beginning in the preadolescent period and following them through to young manhood. After identifying those boys having the highest self-esteem, he compared their childhood influences with those demonstrating a lower sense of self-worth. He found that the high-esteem children were clearly more loved and appreciated at home; the high-esteem group's parents were significantly more strict in their approach to discipline; and the homes of the high-esteem group were characterized by democracy and openness. Once the boundaries for behavior were established, there was freedom for individual personalities to grow and develop.

The Ingredients of Proper Discipline

If good discipline is so important to the building of self-esteem, then, let's discuss its ingredients. Returning to the subject of spanking, when and under what circumstances is it appropriate to use this form of discipline? You will not damage your child emotionally if you follow this philosophy: First, establish boundaries in advance. Tell the child just what the rule is before it is broken. It should be clear what is expected and why. There should be no *ex post facto* guilt.

Second, a child who defiantly challenges authority by disobeying instructions expects you to act. Don't disappoint him. Reserve a spanking for that moment of conflict when the child dares you to defend your right to lead. It should come in response to sassiness, haughtiness, or outright disobedience. *No other form of discipline is as effective as a spanking when willful defiance is involved.* In this sense, corporal punishment is not a "last resort" to be applied after you have screamed,

126

yelled, cried, begged, deprived, wept, and stood the offender in the corner. It is to be used any time a child chooses to stiffen his neck, clench his fists, and toss his little pinkie across the line you've drawn in the dirt.

Third, do not spank for mistakes and accidents. Do not spank for forgetting to feed the dog or make the bed or other acts of immaturity. Do not spank to reinforce lessons. Do not spank today for what was ignored yesterday. This kind of behavior does not represent willful defiance and will be resented.

Fourth, after a spanking, your child will probably want to be loved and reassured. By all means, open your arms and let her come! Hold her close and tell her of your love. Rock her gently and let her know, again, why she was punished and how she can avoid the trouble next time. You cannot talk to a child in this heart-to-heart fashion while you are still in conflict; understanding and closeness are not achieved by sending an angry, defiant child to her room to pout. This moment of communication is created by the emotional ventilation brought on by an appropriate spanking, and it does not destroy self-esteem. It builds love, fidelity, and family unity.

Fifth, your spankings should be completed by the time a child is eight or nine years old. Never spank a teenager. Since the self-concept of an adolescent is in serious doubt anyway, a spanking is the ultimate insult, making an adolescent feel like a baby.

Who's in Charge Here?

Many specialists in child development recommend trying to "reason" the child out of his defiance. Anyone who has ever tried to do that knows it is impossible. Why? Because the issue of "Who's toughest?" is very important to children. Whenever a child moves to a new neighborhood, he often has to fight (verbally or physically) to establish a position on the hierarchy of strength. A teacher will certainly have to defend himself or herself in the first few days of the school year, because the entire class wants to know if the teacher is strong or weak. Regardless of what the parent and child are fighting over, the *real* issue is this: Are you in charge, or am I? And when the stage is set for that battle, reason and explanation simply will not settle the matter.

> *Regardless of what the parent and child are fighting over, the REAL issue is this: Are you in charge, or am I?*

Those same specialists also say that a spanking teaches your child to hit others, making him a more violent person. Nonsense! If your child has ever bumped his arm against a hot stove, you can bet he'll never deliberately do that again. He does not become a more violent person because the stove burned him; in fact, he learned a valuable lesson from the pain. Similarly, when he falls out of his high chair or smashes his finger in the door or is bitten by a grumpy dog, he learns about physical dangers in the world. These bumps and bruises throughout childhood are nature's way of teaching what to fear. They do not damage self-esteem. They do not make vicious people. They acquaint the individual with reality. In like manner, an appropriate spanking from a loving parent provides the same service. It says there are not only physical dangers to be avoided, but one must steer clear of such social traps as selfishness, defiance, dishonesty, and unprovoked aggression.

The Will and the Spirit

I must now return to the original question: Does punishment, particularly spanking, break the spirit of the child? It is very important to understand the difference between breaking the *spirit* of the child and breaking the *will*. The human spirit is exceedingly fragile at all ages and must be handled with care. It involves a person's view of himself, his personal worth, and the emotional factors to which this book is dedicated. A parent can damage a child's spirit very easily— by ridicule, disrespect, threats to withdraw love, and verbal rejection. Anything that depreciates his self-esteem is costly to his spirit. However, while the spirit is brittle and must be treated gently, the will is made of steel. It is full strength at the moment of birth, as any midnight bottle-warmer knows. Even a child whose spirit has been crushed can present the most awesome display of willful power. We want then to shape the will of a child, but leave the spirit intact. This is done by requiring reasonable obedience to predetermined commands and then winning the battle the child chooses to initiate. If you permit your youngster's will to remain unbridled, the result is often extreme self-will, which makes him useless to himself, others, or even to God.

Questions and Answers

Why is there so much confusion on the subject of discipline today? Is it really that difficult to raise our children properly?

Parents are confused because they have been taught an illogical, unworkable approach to child management by many professionals who ought to know better. The authorities on the subject of discipline muddied the water with permissive philosophies that contradict the very nature of children. Let me cite an example. *Growing Pains* is a question-and-answer book for parents published many years ago by the American Academy of Pediatrics, a division of the American Medical Association.[2] The following question from a parent is accompanied by the book's answer:

Q. What does one do when an angry child slams a door in one's face?

A. Step back. Then do nothing until you have reason to believe that the child's anger has cooled off. Trying to reason with an angry person is like hitting your head against a stone wall.

When the child is in a good mood, explain to him how dangerous door-slamming can be. Go so far as to give him a description of how a person can lose a finger from a slammed door. Several talks of this sort are generally enough to cure a door-slammer.

How inadequate this reply is from my point of view. The writer failed to recognize that the door-slamming behavior was not the real issue in this situation. To the contrary, the child was demonstrating defiance of parental authority, and for that should have been held accountable. Instead, the parent is told to wait until the child is in a good mood, which could be next Thursday, and then talk about the dangers of door-slamming. It seems clear that the child was begging Mom to accept the challenge to her authority, but she was in the other room counting to ten and keeping cool. Let's all wish her lots of luck on the next encounter.

As I've stated, the great givers of parental advice have failed to offer a course of action to be applied in response to willful defiance. In the situation described above, for example, what is Mom supposed to do until Junior cools off? What if he is breaking furniture and writing on the back of that slammed door? What if he calls her dirty names and whacks his little sister across the mouth? You see, the *only* tool given to Mom by the writer is postponed *reason*. As every mother knows, reason is practically worthless in response to anger and disrespect.

Nature has provided a wonderfully padded place for use in moments of haughty defiance, and I wish the disciplinary "experts" were less confused as to its proper purpose.

Can you help me better understand the difference between irresponsible and defiant behavior in my children? Why is the distinction important to me as a parent?

The distinction deals with your child's *intention*, which is all-important in knowing how to respond as a parent. Suppose little Johnny is acting silly at the table and spills his milk. He did not intend to knock over the glass, but it happened. Or perhaps he leaves his bicycle out in the rain or loses his schoolbooks. These behaviors result from his childish irresponsibility and should be handled accordingly. It would be wrong to spank a child for being a child, in my view. Rather, these occurrences should offer opportunities to teach him to be more responsible. You may make him work to repair the damage or temporarily deprive him of the item he has abused. However, I feel strongly that a child should never be spanked for mistakes or behaviors he didn't know were wrong, unless it involves a matter of extreme danger (running in the street or invading the medicine cabinet).

By contrast, defiant behavior is very different from childish irresponsibility. It is headstrong and willful. It is premeditated and calculating. In short, it is intentional and deserves immediate disciplinary action.

Perhaps an illustration will help at this point. When my daughter was five years old, she was given a baby hamster for Christmas. Being an incurable animal lover, she became extremely fond of the furry little creature. I noticed at once, however, that she lacked the responsibility to take care of the pet properly. Repeatedly I warned her to keep the door closed on its cage and provide enough food and water for its survival. Despite my intervention, I returned home one day to find my daughter exhausted and red-eyed from crying. Sure enough, she had left the cage door open, and our world-famous dachshund, Siggie (Sigmund Freud), had sent the hamster on to its untimely reward. When my daughter found its stiff, bloody little body near its cage, she was brokenhearted.

What, then, was to be my response? I had told her repeatedly to care for the hamster, but she had failed to do so. Nevertheless, it would have been wrong for me to lash her for this mistake. Instead, I took her in my arms and held her until she stopped crying. Then I talked softly to her in these terms: "Danae, you know that I told you what would happen if you didn't take care of your hamster. But you were thinking about something else, and now he's dead. I'm not mad at you, because you haven't done anything mean. You have just behaved like a child, and I can't blame you for that because you *are* a child. However, I want you to understand something. I warned you about taking care of your hamster because I didn't want to see you get hurt. It was to keep you from feeling like you do today that made me urge you to do the job properly. Now, there will be many other times when I will warn you and teach you and urge you to do something, and I'll also be doing that to keep you from being hurt by life. It is very important for you to see me as your friend, and when I tell you to do something, it is because I love you and can see dangers that you don't see. If you'll learn to listen to what I say, you'll have fewer times like today when you are so sad."

My response to Danae's behavior was dictated by her intention. She did not deliberately defy me, and she deserved no punishment. Likewise, every parent should know individual personalities well enough to make an instantaneous appraisal of this important factor, acting accordingly.

Is it true that the "middle child" has greater problems with low self-esteem than do other members of the family? Maybe that explains why my second son has never been a confident person.

A poor self-concept can become a problem for any human being, regardless of birth order or age. However, you are right that the middle child sometimes finds it more difficult to establish an identity within the family. He enjoys neither the status of the eldest nor the attention given to the baby. He is likely to be born at a busy period in the life of the parents, especially his mother. When he reaches toddler years, his precious territory is invaded by a cute little newborn who steals Mama. Is it any wonder this child often asks, "Who am I? Where is my place in life?"

I recommend that parents take steps to insure the identity of *all* their children, but especially the child in the middle. This can be accomplished by occasionally relating to each boy or girl as an individual, rather than merely as a member of the group. Let me offer two suggestions that may illustrate what I mean:

133

First, ask each offspring to design a personal flag, which can be made from canvas or another fabric. That flag is flown in the front yard on the child's "special" days, including birthdays or after an A in school, a goal in soccer, or a home run in baseball.

Second, it is meaningful for Dad to "date" each child, one at a time, every four or five weeks. The other kids should not be told where they are going until it is revealed by the boy or girl in retrospect. Dad and child can play miniature golf, go bowling, play basketball, eat tacos or pizza, play video games, or visit a skating rink. The choice should be made by the child.

There are other ways to accomplish the same purpose. The target, again, is to plan activities that emphasize one child's individuality, rather than identity within the group.

The children in our neighborhood are so brutal to each other. They ridicule and name-call and fight from morning to night. Is there anything we, as parents, can do about this?

Parents in a neighborhood can bring about a more peaceful atmosphere among their children, *if* they will talk to each other, but that takes some doing. There is no quicker way to anger one mother than for another woman to criticize her precious cub. It is a delicate subject indeed. Thus, the typical neighborhood provides little "feedback" to parents in regard to the behavior of their children. The children know there are no lines of communication among adults, and they take advantage of the barrier. What each block needs is a mother who has the courage to say, "I want to be told what my child does when beyond his own yard. If he is a brat with other children, I would like to know it. If he is disrespectful with adults, please mention it to me. I will not consider it tattling, and I won't resent your coming to me. I hope I can share my insights regarding your children, too. None of our children is perfect, and we'll know better how to teach them if we can talk openly to each other as adults."

Children are capable of learning social skills very early in life, and it is our task to make them "feel" for others.

My little girl is sometimes sugar-sweet, and other times she is unbearably irritating. How can I get her out of a bad mood when she has not really done anything to deserve punishment?

I would suggest that you take her in your arms and talk to her in this manner: "I don't know whether you've noticed it or not, but you have two 'personalities.' A personality is a way of acting and talking and behaving. One of your personalities is sweet and loving. No one could possibly be more lovable and happy when this personality is in control. It likes to work and look for ways to make the rest of the family happy. And all you have to do is press a little button, 'ding,' to call it out. But then sometimes you push another button, 'ding,' and out comes the other personality. It is cranky and noisy and silly. It wants to fight with your brother and disobey your mom. It gets up grouchy in the morning and complains throughout the day. Now, I know that you can press the button for the nice personality or you can call up the mean one. Sometimes it takes a spanking or two to make you press the right button. If you keep on pressing the wrong button, like you have been today, then I'm going to have to make you uncomfortable. I'm tired of that cranky character, and I want to see the grinny one. Can we make a deal?"

When discipline becomes a game, as in a conversation such as this, then you've achieved your purpose without conflict and animosity.

Strategy 7: Keep a Close Eye on the Classroom

What should a parent do when a child is not achieving in school? First, it is necessary to understand that academic failure is a symptom of a more specific cause. There is a great difference, for example, between the underachiever who refuses to work and the slow learner who is *unable* to do what is required. Before we can help the child, therefore, we must diagnose the problem. Most school districts now have school psychologists who will administer a battery of diagnostic tests when needed. Concerned parents can initiate this by calling the guidance office and requesting that an assessment be made. If the local school district does not offer this free service, it might be necessary to seek assistance from a psychologist in private practice.

Once the nature of the difficulty is known, steps can be taken to resolve it. These six suggestions might be helpful:

1. Tutorial assistance can pull a child through a rough spot academically. Particularly in the "three Rs," some children have trouble grasping the concepts while sitting in a classroom. There are too many distractions and too few reasons to concentrate. However, when a tutor can work with a child on a one-to-one basis, learning is much more likely. The school is your best resource in finding a patient, skilled tutor.

2. Be certain your child has learned to read by the end of the second year in school. I'm convinced that self-esteem has more frequently been assassinated over reading problems than by any other aspect of school life. And it is all so unnecessary! Educators have developed many creative approaches to remedial reading—more simplified alphabets, multisensory instruction, and other techniques. Every

child, with *very* few exceptions, can learn to read if taught properly. Unfortunately, however, these techniques are often expensive and may not be provided in your child's classroom. The typical group-teaching approach may be the only program offered, with its high failure rate. Here again, tutorial assistance is strongly recommended. It is absolutely critical to your child's self-confidence to learn to read early in the school career, and if the professional educators can't do the job, someone else must.

3. If you have a confirmed, hard-core "underachiever"—a child who has the ability but absolutely refuses to use it—you have been blessed with a most frustrating academic problem. I'm sure you already knew that. All the screaming, yelling, punishing, crying, and depriving produce little more than a yawn and another F. I have tried many approaches to motivate these happy-go-lucky kids and found most of them to be unsuccessful. The one alternative that has worked has involved a carefully conceived plan of immediate rewards. It is not sufficient, however, to merely bribe a child for working; that produces a short-term fizzle of energy, followed by further apathy. *Dare to Discipline* discusses the principles of reward and reinforcement in considerable detail, specifically as applied to the underachiever. The parent of a child with such a problem may wish to consult that reference.

4. We must deal with the question of what to do for the self-esteem of the slow learner. The question demands an answer because there are so many children in this fix. In the traditional IQ measuring system, intelligence quotients for the total population are distributed around a midpoint of 100. In theory, 50 percent of the children have IQs above 100, and 50 percent score below that point. Obviously, those in the

lower half of the school population are in a high-risk category for learning problems and the self-doubts they bring. The farther down the IQ distribution we go, the more likely we are to find children who face failure daily in the classroom. Approximately 22 percent of children in America have IQs between 70 and 90—intellectual boundaries marking the slow-learner category. Even before they enter first grade it can be predicted that most of these children will soon develop feelings of inadequacy and inferiority. Thus, one-fourth to one-half of our children will eventually enter adult life after twelve years' experience in feeling dumb. They will never forget it.

I offer two strong recommendations to the parents of a slow learner. The first is to de-emphasize academic achievement as a value in your home. This may seem like heresy in an educationally oriented society. However, self-esteem crumbles when the necessary attributes are beyond reach. The importance of anything your child *cannot* accomplish, despite his best efforts, should be toned down. You would not demand that a crippled child become a track star, yet every parent wants his "average" student to become a college graduate. If I had a child with an IQ of 85 who was struggling to do what other children accomplish with ease, I would do my best to remove the pressure from his back. I would concentrate on his strengths and say as little as possible about his unimpressive report card. Some things in life are more important than success in school, and self-esteem is one of them. If forced to choose between these two features, my child's sense of worth will receive higher priority.

The second recommendation is not to allow the school to "fail" a slow learner after kindergarten. I can think of few circumstances that justify retaining an incapable child in the same grade. This creates an image of failure that devastates a child's sense of adequacy. What can he conclude, other than that he is incredibly stupid? All his friends were promoted to the next grade. Why wasn't he? Now look at him, stuck in the same classroom with all the babies! What self-hatred this archaic educational practice has wrought in the lives of its victims. And unfortunately, retention for the slow learner accomplishes nothing academically. This child does not get brighter next year, nor do basic skills suddenly bubble forth. The only thing that changes the second time around is the child's self-concept, which has a sizable crack running from top to bottom.

The slow learner needs parental help in finding compensating skills, coupled with the assurance that personal worth does not depend on success in academia.

5. Another recommendation for the parent of a slow learner is to realize that there are several different kinds of intelligence, not all of which can be measured well by traditional IQ tests. Your child may score a low IQ but be clever mechanically or with spatial relationships. If you can find the particular areas of strength, you will not only be able to boost self-esteem, but you may also be able to use the area of high intelligence to help the student grasp essential school concepts.

Robert Sternberg, a Yale education specialist, identifies three types of students. One has good memory and analytical skills; this child does very well on tests. A second type is quite creative, finding novel solutions to problems, but he or she has trouble functioning within the structure of a standardized test. A third type is "good at everything, excellent at nothing." This child picks up a kind of experiential, street-smart ability.[3]

Harvard professor Howard Gardner identifies seven kinds of intelligence. Linguistic and mathematical intelligence are tested by standard IQ tests. But some have spatial, musical, bodily, interpersonal, or intrapersonal intelligence, he says.[4] This theory is somewhat controversial, because it shakes some traditional assumptions. As *Parents* magazine comments,

> Dr. Gardner's theory amounts to a rethinking of the way we conceive of intelligence, measure intelligence, and encourage its development. Perhaps more important, it is a rethinking of the types of individuals we consider intelligent. In Dr. Gardner's world, an exceptional physicist would not be more brilliant or talented than an exceptional ballerina or poet. A child who was self-aware or sensitive to others would be considered no brighter or duller than one who excelled at writing or music—just talented in a different but equally valid area: And all would be encouraged to develop their abilities.[5]

Most schools still concentrate on linguistic and mathematical abilities. And this is fine, since these are probably the abilities most in demand in our world. Unfortunately, some schools have opted to meet tight budgets by cutting art, music, and sports programs designed to develop spatial, musical, and bodily abilities. Whatever the offerings at school, parents need to find and affirm their own child's areas of greatest strength. Don't ignore the need to improve in weaker areas, but let a child feel successful in some area of life, regardless of what test scores say.

As psychologists Julius and Zelda Segal say, "The mountains of research evidence accumulated on the subject of intelligence convey one message above all: Regardless of the numbers spewed out by IQ tests, each child remains a unique individual with a wellspring of capacities that can flourish over time."[6]

6. There are times when a change of schools—or even a change of teachers within a school—can be in the child's best interest. Educators are reluctant to approve these transfers, for obvious reasons, although the possibility should be considered when the situation demands it. Schools vary tremendously in their difficulty; some are located in higher socioeconomic areas where a majority of the children are much more intelligent than would ordinarily be expected. The mean IQ in schools of this nature may fall between 115 and 120. What happens, then, to a child with average ability in such a setting? Although he may have competed successfully in an ordinary school, he is in the lower 15 percent at Einstein Elementary. Success is not absolute; it is relative. A child does not ask, "How am I doing?" but rather, "How am I doing compared to everyone else?" Little Johnny may grow up thinking himself a dummy when he would have been an intellectual leader in a less competitive setting. Thus, if a child is floundering in one academic environment, the solution may involve a transfer to a more suitable classroom.

The topic of "learning problems" is much too comprehensive to be covered adequately in this brief section. However, the theme running through these comments is important: Parents should be informed regarding the educational progress of their children, intervening appropriately when necessary. Their purpose should be to maximize educational potential without sacrificing self-esteem.

Questions and Answers

Do slow learners and mentally handicapped children have the same needs for esteem that others have?

Sometimes I wish they didn't, but their needs are no different. During a portion of my training at Lanterman State Hospital in California, I was impressed by the vast need for love shown by some of the most retarded patients. There were times when I would step into the door of a children's ward and forty or more severely retarded youngsters would rush toward me screaming, "Daddy! Daddy! Daddy!" They would push and shove around my legs with their arms extending upward, making it difficult for me to avoid falling. Their deep longings to be loved simply couldn't be satisfied in the group experiences of hospital life, despite the exceptionally high quality of Lanterman.

The need for esteem has led me to favor a current trend in education, whereby the borderline mentally retarded children are given special assistance in their regular classrooms without segregating them in special classes. The stigma of being a "retard," as they call themselves, is no less insulting for a ten-year-old than it would be for you or me. In some schools where "mainstreaming" has been successful, other children in the classroom have been instructed ahead of time about the special physical and mental needs of their classmate and are recruited as partners in befriending, encouraging, and assisting the special-needs student.

When I was a child, schools were just getting into something called the "new math." It is my understanding that schools are still teaching some of those concepts. What is your view of it?

The "new math" represented a noble attempt to teach mathematical concepts to children, rather than simply drilling them in mechanical rote processes. The purpose was to help children understand the meaning of math instead of memorizing how to divide, borrow, and count decimal places. I found that approach great for children who had the conceptual power to grasp the principles being taught. Unfortunately, about half the schoolchildren did not possess the ability to handle this abstract reasoning. My concern continues to be for that confused 50 percent. What are we doing for them? With the "old math" they learned how to handle basic computations, even if they didn't understand them all.

I favor a continuation of the effort to challenge mathematically apt students, but we must provide more concrete program alternatives for those students who just don't get the message.

What part does intelligence play in the confidence of adults? Do they tend to forget the trouble they had during the school years?

To the extent that "the boy is the father of the man," we grown-ups are direct products of our own childhood. Thus, everything I have said about self-esteem in children applies to adults as well. We are all graduates of the educational "fail factory," and few have escaped completely unscathed. Further, our self-worth is *still* being evaluated on the basis of intelligence. Dr. Richard Herrnstein, a Harvard University psychologist, predicted several decades ago that a caste system founded on IQ was coming to America, that people would be locked into rigid intellectual classes, which would determine careers, earning power, and social status.

By the late 1980s this process was already being identified. University of Chicago longitudinal education studies showed that class ranking was virtually unchanged from grades three through eleven. Reported *Psychology Today* in 1989,

> Education in this country [the US] is becoming a process of separating the "gifted" from the "average," the "intelligent" from the "slow"—one is tempted to say, the wheat from the chaff. From an early age, children are now ranked and sorted (a process known variably as tracking, ability grouping, or screening) as they proceed through school. Those who test well are encouraged and expected to succeed and offered the most challenging work. Those who do not, get a watered-down curriculum that reflects the system's minimal expectations of them.[7]

Benjamin Bloom, Distinguished Service Professor Emeritus of Education at the University of Chicago, believes that schools are convinced that they can do little to change a student's "learning ability." Thus they begin to see their task as "weeding out the poorer learners, while encouraging the better learners to get as much education as they can." *Psychology Today* cites research by Stanford University professor Henry M. Levin "revealing that placement in a low track has a corroding impact on students' self-esteem. Worse yet, because there are real differences, not just in the level but the *content* of what is being taught, tracking may in fact contribute to academic failure."[8]

While I don't agree fully with all these observations, I do concur that mental ability will be more and more important for self-confidence in this technological world. With both adults and children, we need to begin shoring up this crucial area of self-esteem, which may involve undoing some of the damage done in the educational system.

Strategy 8: Avoid Over-protection and Dependency

Now let's look at the threats to confidence that must come as your child matures. From about three years of age, your little pride and joy begins making his way into the world of other people. Your child plays near home with neighborhood children, is often enrolled in preschool, and a year or two later, will toddle off to kindergarten. Whereas his self-concept could be carefully guarded during the first few years, it now becomes very difficult for you to control the environment. Other children may mock him and laugh at his deficiencies. He may be incapable of competing in their games; or he might even be crippled or killed in an accident of some kind.

This initial "turning loose" period is often extremely threatening to the compulsive mother. Her natural reaction is to hold her baby close to her breast, smothering him in "protection." By watching, guarding, defending, and shielding night and day, perhaps she can spare her child some of the pain she herself experienced growing up. However, her intense desire to help may actually interfere with growth and development. Certain risks must be tolerated if a child is to learn and progress. He will never learn to walk if he is not allowed to fall down in the process.

It is probably easier to foster an unhealthy dependency relationship between parent and child than it is to avoid one. It often begins during the early days of infancy. At the moment of birth, a little child is completely helpless; that little creature lying there can do nothing. She doesn't roll over. She can't scratch her head or verbalize thoughts. She won't lift a finger in her own behalf. Consequently, parents are responsible for meeting every need. They are the infant's servants, and if they're too slow to meet its demands, the baby is equipped with a spine-chilling scream to urge them into action. She bears no obligations whatsoever and doesn't even have to appreciate their efforts. She won't say "please" or "thank you" or apologize for getting them up six times in one night. A child begins life in a state of complete and total dependency.

About twenty years later, however, at the other end of childhood, we expect some radical changes to have occurred. That individual should then be able to assume the full responsibilities of young adulthood. The adult is expected to spend money wisely, hold down a job, be loyal to his or her spouse, support the needs of a family, obey the laws of the land, and be a good citizen. During the course of childhood, an individual should progress from a position of *no* responsibility to a position of *full* responsibility. The question is, how do little John and Joan get from position A to position B? How does this magical transformation of self-discipline take place? There are many self-appointed experts on child raising who seem to feel it all should happen toward the latter end of adolescence, about fifteen minutes before John or Joan leaves home permanently. Prior to that time, the child should be allowed to do whatever is desired at the moment.

I reject that notion categorically. The best preparation for responsible adulthood is training in responsibility during childhood. This is not to say that the child is horsewhipped into acting like an adult. It does mean that the child should be encouraged to progress on an orderly timetable of events, carrying the level of responsibility appropriate for each age. Shortly after birth, for example, the mother begins transferring responsibilities from her shoulders to those of her infant. Little by little he learns to sleep through the night, hold his own bottle, and reach for what he wants. Later he is potty-trained (hopefully) and learns to walk and talk. Gradually, as each new skill is mastered, the mother "frees" herself that much more from servitude.

The best preparation for responsible adulthood is training in responsibility during childhood.

The transfer of responsibility ordinarily runs along smoothly until the child reaches about eighteen months of age. At that point, he suddenly realizes two things: First, work is definitely an evil to be avoided at all costs. He hates the very thought of it. Second, with every new task he is forced to accept, he loses his mama a little more. Previously she was his full-time servant; now she is slipping away. He must pick up his blocks—she isn't going to do it anymore. He must wash behind his ears—she won't be there to wield the washcloth next time. And at this age he craves adult attention. Therefore, if he is going to retain his playmate, he'd better keep her on the job. His thoughts are not this conscious or rational, of course, but anyone who has ever raised a toddler knows it happens. Consequently, a great tug-of-war ensues. Mom is trying to get Junior to grow up, and he's trying to maintain his infancy.

Enter again the emotional and physical threats of which I've spoken. They can easily cause an anxious mother to turn loose the rope in the tug-of-war. Her idea is: "If I keep him dependent on me as long as possible, I can better protect him from the cruel world." Therefore, she won't let him cross the street for several years after he could make it safely. She does *everything,* requiring nothing in return. She enters into each neighborhood argument that occurs among his friends, taking his side regardless of who was right. Later she walks him to school, holding his hand with the proud assurance that she is being a good mother. And heaven help the teacher who tries to discipline her little tiger! All through childhood she fosters a continuation of the infancy relationship, retaining all the responsibility on her back.

Does Junior prosper under this setup? Of course not. Mother is giving of herself totally, which seems a loving thing to do. However, at the same time she is allowing her overprotected child to fall behind in the normal timetable in preparation for ultimate release as a young adult. As a ten-year-old he can't make himself do anything unpleasant, since he never has had any experience in handling the difficult. He does not know how to "give" to someone else, for he has only thought of himself. He finds it hard to make decisions or to exercise self-discipline. A few years later he will be an adolescent completely unprepared for freedom and responsibility. His future spouse is in for some surprises I shudder to contemplate. Marguerite and Willard Beecher, authors of an excellent book called *Parents on the Run,* first described the concept this scenario presents.[9] They stated, and I strongly agree, that the parent must gain freedom from the child so that the child can gain freedom from the parent. Think about that for a moment. If you never get free from your child by transferring responsibility, then the child remains hopelessly bound to you as well. You have knotted each other in a paralyzing interdependency that stifles growth and development.

One young widow had been left with the terrifying task of raising a baby by herself. Davie was the only person left in the world she really loved. Her reaction was to smother him totally. The boy was seven years old when she came to me. He was afraid to sleep in a room by himself. He refused to stay with a babysitter and even resisted going to school. He did not dress himself, and his behavior was infantile in every regard. In fact, instead of waiting in the reception room while I talked to his mother, he found my office and stood with his hand on the doorknob for an hour, whimpering and begging to be admitted. His mother interpreted all this as evidence of his fear that she would die as his father had. In response, she bound him even more tightly, sacrificing all her own needs and desires. She could neither go on dates nor bring any men into their home. She could not get involved in any activities of her own or have any adult experiences without her cling-along son. She had never gained her freedom from Davie, and Davie had not gained his freedom from his lovin' mama.

Have you allowed your child to enjoy age-appropriate freedom and responsibility? Does your fear of emotional and physical hardships keep a child locked in your arms? Are you afraid to make him work because he protests so loudly? I have discovered that this process of dependency may not always be motivated by an admirable desire to protect the child. Very often, a mother (more frequently than the father) will foster a binding relationship to meet her own emotional needs. Perhaps the romance has gone out of her marriage, and a child is her only real source of love. Perhaps she has had trouble making lasting friendships. For whatever reason, she wants to remain at the center of the life of her child. I'm certain Davie's mom had this need. Thus, the parent fosters dependence, waiting on the child hand and foot. She refuses to obtain her freedom for the specific purpose of denying him his. I know one mother-daughter team that maintained this interlocutory relationship until the mother's death at ninety-four years of age. The daughter, then seventy-two, found herself unmarried, alone, and on her own for the first time. It's a frightening thing to experience in old age what other people endure in adolescence.

As indicated, this vital task of turning a child loose is not restricted to the early years. It is equally important all the way through the march toward young adulthood. Each year a child should make more decisions. More routine responsibilities of living should fall on his shoulders as he is able to handle them. A seven-year-old, for example, is usually capable of selecting clothing for the day, making the bed each morning, and keeping a bedroom straight. A nine- or ten-year-old may carry more freedom, such as the choice of television programs to watch (within reason). I am not suggesting abdicating parental leadership. I believe we should give conscious thought to the reasonable, orderly transfer of freedom and responsibility so that we are preparing the child each year for that moment of full independence. The twenty-year process of "letting go" is diagrammed below, with examples of independence to be added at each level.

Now I have a very important message at this point, of particular relevance to Christian parents. Others are invited to read along, but you may not comprehend its full significance. I have observed that the process of "letting go" during late adolescence is much more difficult for parents with deep religious convictions than for those without them. Christian families are more likely to be aware of, and be concerned by,

BIRTH
(no responsibility)

Sleeps through the night

Holds own bottle

Sits up, crawls

Learns to walk

Tug-of-war during toddler years → Obeys simple instructions

Is toilet trained

Picks up toys and blocks

Helps with household tasks

Feeds dog regularly

Maintains an allowance

Does homework without being rewarded

(Duration of Childhood)

Chooses own clothes

Baby-sits with young child

Has a paper route

Has first date

Curfew extended an hour

Has a regular Saturday job

Dates whom he chooses

Greater freedom with car

Completion of "transfer" → Spends money as wishes

Sets own hours to be in

Few decisions required—
great independence

Release from home

Final release from parental
responsibility

YOUNG ADULTHOOD

(full responsibility)

the spiritual dangers their children will face with increasing independence and freedom. They have greater reason to fear the consequences of premarital intercourse, marriage to a nonbeliever, rejection of the Christian ethic, and other departures from the faith they have taught. Everything they have said during the first eighteen years will either be incorporated into the values of the new adult, or it will be all rejected and thrown overboard. The importance of this decision, then, causes too many zealous parents to hold on tightly to their maturing child. They insist that he do what is right, demanding his obedience and loyalty. They allow him to make few important decisions and try to force-feed certain attitudes. But the day for that kind of programming is past. The result is often tremendous resentment in the adolescent, leading to defiance just to prove independence.

A mother with this "hang-on" attitude came to me recently in regard to her twenty-year-old son, Paul. He was not obeying her as she thought he should, and the conflict was literally making her sick. Paul rented an apartment against her will, with a roommate she disliked, and he was seen with girls of questionable reputation. He threatened to transfer from a Christian college to a local university and more or less denounced his faith.

"What can I do? What can I possibly do to get him straightened out?" she asked.

I told her that Paul's day-to-day behavior was no longer her responsibility. She had completed her task as his mother and should set him free. I explained that her nagging and begging were probably accentuating Paul's defiance, since she was playing an inappropriate "mothering" role he resented. I suggested that this woman sit down and write her son a polite and loving letter, telling him emphatically that she was letting him go—once and for all.

Several days later the woman brought for my approval a rough draft of a letter she had written. It was not what I had in mind. Her composition turned out to be a finger-wagging indictment, warning of the future and urging the wayward boy back to his senses. It was impossible to edit what she had written, so I wrote a letter for her. She sent my letter to her son over her own signature, and I have printed it below with her permission:

Dear Paul:

This is the most important letter I have ever written to you, and I hope you will take it as seriously as it is intended. I have given a great amount of thought and prayer to the matter I want to convey and believe I am right in what I've decided to do.

For the past several years, you and I have been involved in a painful tug-of-war. You have been struggling to free yourself of my values and my wishes for your life. At the same time, I have been trying to hold you to what we both know is right. Even at the risk of nagging, I have been saying, "Go to church," "Choose the right friends," "Make good grades in school," "Live a Christian life," "Prepare wisely for your future," etc. I'm sure you've gotten tired of this urging and warning, but I have only wanted the best for you. This is the only way I knew to keep you from making some of the mistakes so many others have made.

However, I've thought all of this over during the last month, and I believe that my job as your mother is now finished. Since the day you were born, I have done my best to do what was right for you. I have not always been successful—I've made mistakes, and I've failed in many ways. Someday you will learn how difficult it is to be a good parent, and perhaps then you'll understand me better than you do now. But there's one area where I have never wavered: I've loved you with everything that is within me. It is impossible to convey the depth of my love for you through these years, and that affection is as great today as it's ever been. It will continue to be there in the future, although our relationship will change from this moment. As of now, you are free! You may reject God or accept Him, as you choose. Ultimately, you will answer only to Him anyway. You may marry whomever you wish without protest from me. You may go to UCLA or USC or any other college of your selection. You may fail or succeed in each of life's responsibilities. The umbilical cord is now broken.

I am not saying these things out of bitterness or anger. I still care what happens to you and am concerned for your welfare. I will pray for you daily, and if you come to me for advice, I'll offer my opinion. *But the responsibility now shifts from my shoulders to yours.* You are a man now, and you're entitled to make your own decisions—regardless of the consequences. Throughout your life I've tried to build a foundation of values that would prepare you for this moment of manhood and independence. That time has come, and my record is in the books.

I have confidence in you, son. You are gifted and have been blessed in so many ways. I believe God will lead you and guide your footsteps, and I am optimistic about the future. Regardless of the outcome, I will always have a special tenderness in my heart for my beloved son.

Sincerely,
Your mother

This message simply must be conveyed to your child when the time comes, whether it be discussed in conversation or written in the form of a letter. We are given eighteen or twenty years to interject the proper values and attitudes; then we must take our hands off and trust in divine leadership to influence the outcome. And surprisingly, the chances of a young adult making the right decisions are greatly increased when no fight is underway for adulthood and independence.

The biblical story of the Prodigal Son in Luke 15:11–32 is a brilliant guide to follow at this point. The father knew his boy was going to squander his money and live with prostitutes. He knew he would make many mistakes and possibly destroy himself in the process. Yet he permitted the young man to leave home. He did not chain him to a tree or even condemn him verbally. Nor did he bail him out when he ran aground in the distant land. The love with which the father said good-bye made it possible for his son to return after making a mess of his life. We would do well to follow the father's loving example.

Our final task in building self-esteem for our children comes as we transfer responsibility from our shoulders to theirs, beginning with the rudimentary skills of infancy and terminating with their emancipation during the late teens or early twenties. Letting go is not an easy task, but good parenthood demands it.

Questions and Answers

How can I teach my fourteen-year-old the value of money?

One good technique is to give him enough cash to meet a particular need, and then let him manage it. You can begin by offering a weekly food allowance to be spent in school. If he squanders the total on a weekend date, then it becomes his responsibility to either work for his lunches or go hungry. This is the cold reality he will face in later life, and it will not harm him to experience the lesson while still an adolescent.

I should note that this principle has been known to backfire. A physician friend of mine has four daughters, and he provided each with an annual clothing allowance when they turned twelve years old. It then became the girls' responsibility to budget their money for the garments needed throughout the year. The last child to turn twelve, however, was not quite mature enough to handle the assignment. She celebrated her twelfth birthday by buying an expensive coat, which cut deeply into her available capital. The following spring she exhausted her funds totally and wore shredded socks, holey underwear, and frayed jeans for the last three months of the year. It was difficult for her parents not to intervene, but they had the courage to let her learn this valuable lesson about money management.

Perhaps your son has never learned the value of money because it comes too easily. Anything in abundant supply becomes rather valueless. I would suggest that you restrict the pipeline and maximize the responsibility required in all expenditures.

We have a very flighty, bouncy, eight-year-old boy who cringes at the thought of work. His room is always a disaster area, and he can sit and look at a job for hours without finishing it. How can we teach him to be more responsible?

Your son has a lot of company among eight-year-olds, most of whom get depressed over the very thought of work. Nevertheless, it is not too early to begin teaching him the meaning of self-discipline. I would suggest that you follow this plan:

1. Early tomorrow morning, sit down with your son and tell him that you are going to begin teaching him how to work, because that is one of your jobs as a parent. Perhaps you will want to read to him Proverbs 6:6–11, where the value of work is described.

2. Take him on a tour of his "pig pen," showing him how messy he's been. All this discussion is to be done without finger-wagging and accusations. It's just a matter of fact that the time has come to learn something new.

3. List and post his daily jobs in his room. Spell out exactly what will be expected from him. Let him help select the jobs he will assume, equaling about one hour of work per day.

4. For a confirmed goof-off, you will need to capitalize on every ounce of motivational power that can possibly be generated. Therefore, you must use the two things that will "move" kids: There must be something to gain for doing this job and something to lose for doing it wrong. The greater the distance between these two alternatives, the more willing he will be to accept new responsibility. For example, I would construct an eight-inch thermometer, as illustrated below:

$5.00	5 hrs.
$4.00	4 hrs.
$3.00	3 hrs.
$2.00	2 hrs.
$1.00	1 hr.

Down the left-hand side is the rate at which the child will be paid for work. Set the fee at whatever level is appropriate for a child his age. Down the right-hand side is listed the time factor, or number of hours worked. Each day, the "employee" fills in the thermometer with a yellow or red pen, moving upward toward a set goal. At the top is a picture of the objective, such as a CD recording, a computer game, a fishing reel, or anything that the child wants badly.

For many irresponsible children, a second system must accompany the first: There must be a reason not to reject the offer, making use of both positive and negative reinforcement. To accomplish this purpose, tell your child: "I have worked out this thermometer plan to help you enjoy working, because I don't want you to be miserable. But you don't have the choice of accepting or rejecting it. One way or the other, I am going to teach you how to work. If I don't do that, I will fail in one of my most important jobs as a parent. So here is our bargain. Your Saturdays are entirely free. You don't have to do any work on Saturday, provided you complete your jobs properly during the five weekdays. Each day that you fail to do the things on your list, though, will be made up on Saturday, without pay. You see, if you do nothing five days a week, you'll owe me five hours of free labor on Saturday. If you get your work done all week, you get paid, and Saturday is yours. You choose which way it will be."

Three things are essential to make this system work. The absence of any one of the three will blow the entire game:

1. Don't nag and plead and push. The responsibility is your child's, not yours. One simple reminder might be appropriate, but the goal is to get results on personal initiative. Discuss this in the beginning.

2. When the child fails without excuse, be hard-nosed about the Saturday makeup time. This should be an extremely painful experience. If you fold up at this point and fail to follow through, you've lost the future motivational power from this negative reinforcement.

3. Make sure the goal at the top of the thermometer is something your child wants badly. Once the goal is reached, get the reward immediately.

There will be those who oppose this kind of structured program, preferring that the child work for the sheer love of work. I wish every child was noble enough to carry responsibility without outside pressure or reward. The truth is that some children will do nothing for eighteen years unless they are programmed into a structure having only one way out, the door of responsibility. If you have such a child, you must either plan such a program or resign yourself to sloppy procrastination.

Strategy 9: Teach Children to Be Kind

What *one* change in Western culture could produce a higher percentage of emotionally healthy children and adults? This is a stimulating question that might draw differing answers from professionals. From my perspective, the most valuable revision would be for adults to begin actively teaching children, by precept and personal example, to love and respect each other.

Far from manifesting kindness and sensitivity, children are often permitted to be terribly brutal and destructive, especially to the disabled child, the unattractive child, the slow-learning child, the uncoordinated child, the foreign child, the minority child, the small or large child, and the child who is perceived to be different in even the most insignificant feature. Predictably, the damage inflicted on young victims often reverberates for a lifetime.

Emotional problems usually originate in at least one of two kinds of rejection: The relationship with parents was unloving or unnourishing, and/or the individual could not gain acceptance and respect from peers. Most nonorganic emotional disorders can be traced to destructive relationships during the first twenty years of life. If this is true, then adults should devote their creative energies to the teaching of *love* and *dignity*. And if necessary, we should insist that children approach each other with kindness. Can boys and girls be taught to respect their peers? They certainly can! Young people are naturally more sensitive and empathetic than adults. Viciousness is a learned response, resulting from the highly competitive and hostile world their leaders have permitted to develop. Children are destructive to the weak and lowly because we adults haven't bothered to teach them to "feel" for one another.

Perhaps a comparison of two school classes will illustrate my concern. As noted earlier, some mainstreaming programs have successfully integrated learning disabled children into classrooms by training fellow students in kindness. In one model program elementary and middle school students have annual "workshops" on disabilities and how they can help. Then they are acquainted with the particular disabilities of the special education student(s) who will be joining their class. Two volunteers are "trained" to be the new child's special friends. In one case a girl with severe epilepsy and mild retardation was mainstreamed into a middle school classroom. Class members learned how to protect this child during seizures and what to do during her drastic mood swings. Each member of the class became fiercely loyal to their own classmate and to the special education students in other classes. Sometimes students became involved in special tutoring. Anyone foolish enough to make fun of one of these kids soon stood eyeball-to-eyeball against every other kid in the class. Acceptance of others increased noticeably throughout the classes involved, and relationships formed with the special education students that continued through high school.

A more negative example was reported by a room mother for her daughter's fourth-grade class. This room mother assisted the teacher with the traditional Valentine's Day party. Valentine's Day can be the most painful day of the year for an unpopular child, and many schools have either discontinued the exchanging of valentines or set rules that children cannot give selectively to some classmates and not others. Students do count the number of valentines they receive as a measure of social worth. At this party the teacher announced that the class was going to play a game with boy-girl teams. That was her first mistake, since fourth graders have not yet experienced the happy hormones that draw the sexes together. The moment the teacher instructed the students to select a partner, all the boys immediately laughed and pointed at the homeliest and least respected girl in the room. She was overweight, had protruding teeth, and was too withdrawn even to look anyone in the eye.

"Don't put us with Hayley," they all said in mock terror. "Anybody but Hayley! She'll give us a disease! Ugh! Spare us from Horrible Hayley." The mother waited for the teacher, a strong disciplinarian, to rush to the aid of the beleaguered little girl. But to her disappointment, nothing was said to the insulting boys. Instead, the teacher left Hayley to cope with the painful situation in solitude.

Ridicule by one's own sex is distressing, but rejection by the opposite sex is like taking a hatchet to the self-concept. What could the devastated child say in reply? How does an overweight fourth-grade girl defend herself against nine aggressive boys? What response could she make but to blush in mortification and slide foolishly into her chair? The child, whom God loves more than the possessions of the entire world, will never forget that moment, or the teacher who abandoned her in this time of need.

Children are destructive to the weak and lowly because we adults haven't bothered to teach them to "feel" for one another.

Had I been the teacher of Hayley's class on that fateful Valentine's Day, those mocking, joking boys would have had a fight on their hands. Of course, it would have been better if the embarrassment could have been prevented by discussing the feelings of others from the first day of school. But if the conflict occurred as described, with Hayley's ego suddenly shredded for everyone to see, I would have thrown the full weight of my authority and respect on her side of the battle.

My spontaneous response would have carried this general theme: "Wait just a minute! By what right do any of you boys say such mean, unkind things to Hayley? I want to know which of you is so perfect that the rest of us couldn't make fun of you in some way? I know you all very well. I know about your homes and your school records and some of your personal secrets. Would you like me to share them with the class, so we can all laugh at you the way you just did at Hayley? I could do it! I could make you want to crawl in a hole and disappear. But listen to me! You need not fear. I will never embarrass you in that way. Why not? Because it *hurts* to be laughed at by your friends. It hurts even more than a stubbed toe or a cut finger or a bee sting.

"I want to ask those of you who were having such a good time a few minutes ago: Have you ever had a group of children make fun of you in the same way? If you haven't, then brace yourself. Some day it will happen to you, too. Eventually you will say something foolish ... and they'll point at you and laugh in your face. And when it happens I want you to remember what happened today.

"Class, let's make sure that we learn something important from what took place here this afternoon. First, we will not be mean to each other in this class. We will laugh together when things are funny, but we will not do it by making one person feel bad. Second, I will never intentionally embarrass anyone in this class. You can count on that. Each of you is a child of God. He molded you with His loving hands, and He has said that we all have equal worth as human beings. This means that Michael is neither better nor worse than Brian or Molly or Brent. Sometimes I think maybe you believe a few of you are more important than others. It isn't true. Every one of you is priceless to God, and each of you will live forever in eternity. That's how valuable you are. God loves each boy and girl in this room, and because of that, I love every one of you. He wants us to be kind to other people, and we're going to practice that kindness through the rest of this year."

When a strong, loving teacher comes to the aid of the least respected child in the class, as I've described, something dramatic occurs in the emotional climate of the room. Every child seems to utter an audible sigh of relief. The same thought is bouncing around in many heads: "If Hayley is safe from ridicule—even overweight Hayley—then I must be safe, too." By defending the least popular child, a teacher is demonstrating that there are no "pets." Everyone is respected by the teacher, and the teacher will fight for anyone who is treated unjustly. Children highly value those three virtues, which contribute to mental health.

I also suggest to parents that you be quick to defend the underdog in your neighborhood. Let it be known that you have the confidence to speak for the outcast. Explain this philosophy to your neighbors, and try to create an emotional harbor for the little children whose ship has been threatened by a storm of rejection. Don't be afraid to exercise leadership on behalf of a youngster who is being mauled. No other investment of your time and energy is more worthy.

This message is especially important for Christian parents, whose children need to learn empathy and kindness during the early years. After all, Jesus gave the highest priority to the expression of love for God and for our neighbor, yet we often miss the emphasis in Christian education. For example, many Sunday schools diligently teach about Moses and Daniel and Joseph but permit a chaotic classroom where cavorting students mutilate one another's egos. In fact, when a Sunday school lacks strong leadership as I've described, it can become the most "dangerous" place in a child's week. That's why I like to see the church workers spring to the defense of a harassed underdog, and in so doing, speak volumes about human worth and the love of Jesus.

To be honest, I wonder why this suggestion is necessary. I find it difficult to comprehend why adults have to be encouraged to shield a vulnerable child whose defenses have crumbled. What strange inhibition makes a loving teacher stand immobile while self-esteem is being assassinated in an overweight fourth-grade girl? Why will car pool drivers ignore brutal attacks collectively hurled at the least popular rider? Why do mothers permit siblings to engage in emotional sabotage, with little more than a whimpered request for peace and quiet? Somehow, we adults feel we don't have a right to intervene in the antagonistic world of children. Well, it is my opinion that we *do* have the right; indeed we have an obligation to say, "Let it be understood that we *will not* treat one another with disrespect in this house, period! The deliberate violator of that rule will face certain unpleasant consequences." Children will welcome this requirement, even while they are attempting to disobey it.

Let me conclude by emphasizing that our failure as a culture to teach our children to be kind appears to be partially responsible for the wave of youth violence occurring today. In nearly every instance of random violence on school campuses, young perpetrators who shoot their classmates have been ridiculed and harassed by their peers. That was the case at Columbine High School in Littleton, Colorado, on that tragic afternoon in April 1999. Twelve students and a teacher were murdered before the two seventeen-year-old gunmen committed suicide. While they bear the full blame for the massacre, one cannot examine the underlying circumstances without seeing evidence of rejection by the more popular kids. Anger apparently accumulated and then found expression in the Goth scene, which teaches death, violence, and sexual perversion. Similar experiences occur in many other students who resort to retaliation and murder.

We must identify the children and teenagers who harbor deep resentment and seek professional help for them. But first, our obligation as parents and guardians is to teach kids to respect one another and to defend those who are particularly vulnerable. It is our profound obligation to get this done.

7

Help the Teenager Succeed

I would be hard pressed to say whether the stresses of the teen years are more difficult for the youngster or for other members of his or her family. This period offers something painful for everyone. But there are ways to minimize its impact.

Why is adolescence so discouraging? Most teenagers do not fully understand what is happening to them. There are rapid changes in their bodies and feelings and in the bodies and feelings of their friends. This makes them especially vulnerable to feelings of inferiority. Much of their fear, anxiety, and discouragement could be lessened by implementing some of the suggestions offered in the following section.

Strategy 10: Prepare for Adolescence

All of childhood is a preparation for adolescence and beyond. Mothers and fathers are granted a single decade to lay
a foundation of values and attitudes by which their children
cope with the pressures and problems of adulthood. As such,
we would all do well to acquaint our young children with
the meaning of self-worth and its preservation, since every
human being has to deal with that issue at some point in
the life cycle.

This teaching process should begin during the kindergarten years, if not before. For example, when your child meets
someone who is shy you might say, "Why do you suppose
Billie is too embarrassed to tell you what she is feeling? Do
you think she doesn't have much self-confidence?" Use the
word *confidence* frequently, referring to a kind of courage and
belief in one's self. When your child participates in a school or
church program, compliment him for having the confidence
to stand in front of a group.

Then, as the elementary years unfold, begin focusing on
the negative side of that important ingredient. Talk openly
about feelings of inferiority and what they mean. For example,
"Did you notice how David acted so silly in class this morning? He was trying hard to make everyone pay attention to
him, wasn't he? Do you have any idea why he needs to be
noticed every minute of the day? Maybe it's because David
doesn't like himself very much. I think he is trying to force
people to like him because he thinks he is disrespected. Why
don't you try to make friends with David and help him feel
better about himself? Would you like to invite him to spend
the night?"

Not only will you help your child "tune in" to the feelings of others through this instruction, but you will also be teaching self-understanding of feelings of inadequacy. Each year that passes should bring more explicit understanding of the crises in worth that come to everyone. Give your child illustrations of people who have overcome great feelings of inferiority. Several are mentioned in this book. But the best examples will come from the struggles of your own adolescence.

During the child's tenth year, or certainly no later than the eleventh, it would be wise for the mother or father to schedule a weekend trip with that child. Parent and child should go to the beach or to the mountains or to a local resort where they will not be disturbed. It would probably be best for fathers to talk to sons and mothers to talk to daughters, although the opposite sexes may communicate better in some families. Certainly

All of childhood is a preparation for adolescence and beyond. Mothers and fathers are granted a single decade to lay a foundation of values and attitudes by which their children cope with the pressures and problems of adulthood.

in single-parent homes this outing is especially important. Depending on the dynamics of the relationships, it may be a good time for the noncustodial parent to interact with the child to show continuing solidarity. Or the custodial parent can make it a special time alone with the child, with friends caring for siblings for the weekend.

Those three days together would be devoted to an explanation of the adolescent experience. The conversations should involve much more than the laughable "birds-and-bees" talk, which usually degenerates to a tension-filled, sweaty-palmed discussion about reproductive facts the child has known for at least three years. Rather, I recommend that parents present a carefully planned panorama of the physical, emotional, and social changes that are rapidly approaching. Careful notes should be taken during the course of the weekend. The parent should write down each point that has been made regarding the remarkable changes that will be occurring in the child's body, the new social demands, tensions that are likely to develop between generations, and how it is all part of growing up and becoming independent. A list should be made of misconceptions common to teens and areas of greatest concern. The discussion should pause at the spiritual confusion that often occurs in adolescence and focus on occupational and career choices the child must eventually make.

The purpose for dutifully recording the gist of these conversations is that the child is not going to remember much of what was said. The words of the parent will quietly slip away during the years that follow. If the notes are kept in an accessible place until needed, several years later, when the teen is discouraged and distressed and rejected and lovesick and emotional and anxious, the paper can be retrieved. If each child keeps a personal file in the family computer, a copy of the notes can be readily available, and the teen will be reminded of the conversation each time the file is opened to do homework or work on other projects. A lot of advice will be only a couple of clicks of the mouse away. Keep a backup copy in case the original gets trashed in a moment of adolescent wrath.

These notes are most helpful at moments of crisis, when a carefully timed follow-up discussion can be initiated. The parent can show the relevant notes and say, "You see, each thing you're experiencing was anticipated several years ago. It was predictable, for it is all part of the transition from childhood to adulthood." Then the parent can point to the last item on the final page, which reads: "Normality *will* return!" Just as surely as these upsetting events were accurately predicted, their end can also be forecast with certainty.

If the trials of adolescence can be viewed as a temporary phase through which everyone must pass, then the distress is tolerable. But the natural inclination of an immature mind is to see today as forever. "My situation is awful, and it will never change. There is no way out. There are no solutions and no one understands." These explosive thoughts can be defused by a caring parent.

There is one hitch in the recommendation above. A parent who would teach about adolescence must first know the subject. Invariably, when I have proposed this instructional program to groups of parents, they have asked for more information about what discussions with the preteen should include. The following section addresses primarily that topic. Intermingled with this description are related suggestions for the teen years. You may want to read some passages from the next pages to your child or structure your own approach around these points.

What Is Adolescence?

The term *adolescence* is familiar, yet its definition is frequently misunderstood. It is *not* a physical term, as such. It does not mean "the time of life when a child matures sexually."

That is the definition of "puberty." *Adolescence* is a cultural term, meaning the age between childhood and adulthood in a particular society. It is the period when an individual has neither the privileges of childhood nor the freedoms of adulthood.

The length of adolescence varies remarkably from one society to another. In some people groups there is no adolescence at all. One day a pubescent boy or girl is treated as a child—allowed to play and expected to follow the wishes of parents. The next day there is a traditional rite of puberty, perhaps including a night alone in the forest in pursuit of a mythical animal. Following that rite the individual is treated as a full-fledged man or woman, fighting in battle, working with other adults, and enjoying the status and respect of maturity. There is no in-between phase for these young people.

By contrast, the Western world has the longest period of adolescence in the history of humanity. Herein lies much of the related discontent. For an intolerably long period, children are without status and respect. They resent their plight, and I can understand their frustration. For the fifteen-year-old, everything "adult" is forbidden. Driver's training may allow a taste of automotive freedom, but driving is very restricted. So is the number of hours one can be officially "working." The fifteen-year-old cannot marry, enlist, borrow, drink (legally), make many personal decisions, vote, or join a labor union. Sexual desires are denied gratification during a period of greatest excitation. The only alternative is to continue in school, whether one likes it or not. We as adults know it must be this way, yet the teenager often interprets prohibitions as evidence of disrespect.

This in-between age usually lasts as long as the individual remains financially dependent upon parents. Thus, in some cases, a twenty-five-year-old graduate student has not been granted complete adult status by parental benefactors. Ordinarily, however, adolescence lasts from age thirteen to twenty-one in males and from twelve to twenty-one in females. It can terminate earlier if marriage occurs or education is interrupted. Obviously, nine or ten years is a long time to be disenfranchised by a society, accounting for some of the rebellion of the period.

Knowing that adolescents often chafe under their lack of status in the adult world, I would offer this very important suggestion to the parents of a teenager: Treat him with genuine respect and dignity. Let your manner convey your acceptance of him as an individual, even aiming your conversation a year or two above his head. Does this mean you have to pussyfoot when he has defied your authority or overstepped reasonable boundaries? Certainly not. It is possible to treat a child respectfully, even when punishment is necessary. In fact, during my years as a schoolteacher—at times seeing 225 teenagers in my classroom each day—I learned that youngsters will tolerate all sorts of rules and restrictions, provided you don't assault their egos. But if you make them feel childish and foolish, brace yourself for hostility. Much of the strife between generations could be eliminated if relationships were mixed generously with mutual respect.

Let's examine other subjects that should be discussed with a child during the months immediately preceding adolescence.

Adolescence Is an Age of Dramatic Physical Change

Every preteen should be informed of the rapid physical changes about to occur. For the adult who has ever lost sleep over an unidentified lump or other suspicious symptom, it is easy to imagine how a youngster feels when everything goes haywire all at once. I have found that uninformed teenagers fall into two broad categories: The first group didn't know the physical changes were coming and are worried sick by what they see happening. The second group is aware that certain features are supposed to appear and are anxious because the changes are late in arriving. Whether your child is voicing fears or not, scores of tense questions are being asked: Does this pain in my breasts mean I have cancer? Why do I feel tired all the time? The older boys have hair down below; why don't I? Am I normal? Will I always look like a baby? Why do I have cramps and pain in my stomach? Could I bleed to death? What is happening to my voice? The doubts and fears are endless, yet they could be avoided by healthy, confident parental instruction. Listed below are some of the subjects that should be discussed in anticipation of adolescence:

1. Rapid growth will sap energy and strength for a while. The teenager will actually need more sleep and better nutrition than at a younger age.
2. The child's body will quickly change to that of an adult. Sex organs will become more mature and will be surrounded by pubic hair. For males, stress that the size of the penis is of no physical importance. Many boys worry tremendously about having a smaller organ, but that has nothing to do with fathering a child or sexual satisfaction as an adult. For females, breast development can be discussed in the same manner.
3. Full details of the menstrual cycle must be made clear to your daughter before her first period. It is

a terrifying thing for a girl to experience this aspect of maturity without forewarning. Many books and films are available to help explain this developmental milestone and should be used. The most important parental responsibility is to convey confidence, optimism, and excitement regarding menstruation, rather than saying sadly, "This is the cross you must bear as a woman."

4. The timing of puberty must be discussed, for herein lies much grief and distress. This period of heightened sexual development may occur as early as twelve or as late as nineteen years of age in boys and from ten to seventeen in girls. Thus, it may arrive seven years earlier in some children than in others. And the youngsters who develop very early or very late usually face some upsetting psychological problems.

Four extremes of timing should be considered:

The late-maturing boy knows perfectly well that he is still a baby while his friends have grown up. He picks up the telephone, and the person on the other end calls him "ma'am"! What an insult! He's very interested in athletics, but he can't compete with the larger, stronger boys. He gets teased in the locker room about his sexual immaturity, and his self-esteem nose-dives. Adding insult to injury, he is actually shorter than most of the girls for a couple of years. They have had their growth spurt, and he has not. He fears something is drastically wrong, but he dares not mention his thoughts to anyone. It's too embarrassing. This prepubertal child can often be the worst troublemaker in the school, for he feels he has many things to prove about his doubtful manhood.

Life is no easier for *the late-maturing girl*, whose internal clock also is on the slow side. She looks down at her flat chest and then glances at her busty friends. For two or three years her girlfriends have been sharing confidences about menstruation, but she can't participate in the discussions. She has been nicknamed "baby face" by her friends, and in fact she does look about eight years old. Given the role physical attractiveness plays in self-esteem, inferiority can overwhelm the late developer, even if he or she is attractively arranged. And unless someone tells them otherwise, they are likely to conclude that they will never grow up.

If it is disadvantageous to be late in maturing, one would think that the opposite would be emotionally healthy. Not so. Since girls tend to develop sexually one or two years before boys on average, *the early-maturing girl* is miles ahead of everyone else her age. Physical strength offers her no real advantages in our society, and it is simply not acceptable to be boy-crazy at ten years of age. For two or three uncomfortable years, the early-maturing girl is out of step with all her age-mates.

The early-maturing boy is blessed with a great social advantage. He is strong at a time when power is worshiped by his peers, and his confidence soars as his athletic successes are publicized. His early development places him on a par with the girls in his class, who also are awakening sexually. Thus, he has the field all to himself for a year or two. Research confirms that the early-maturing boy is more frequently emotionally stable, confident, and socially accepted than other boys. It also shows that he is more likely to be successful in later adult life.

In the discussion of these extremes with a preteenager, stress that it is "normal" for some youngsters to be early or late in developing. It does not mean anything is wrong. The late bloomer will need additional reassurance and encouragement in the years ahead. Finally, an attempt should be made at the time of this conversation to open the door of communication regarding the fears and anxieties associated with physical growth and development.

Incidentally, I should mention one more aspect of adolescent physiology before moving on. Statistical records indicate that children are taller than in the past, probably the result of better nutrition, medicine, exercise, rest, and recreation. This additional stature has produced the interesting consequence that sexual maturity is occurring at younger ages. Apparently, puberty in a particular child is activated at a certain level of growth. Therefore, when environmental circumstances propel a child upward at a faster rate, sexual maturity also begins earlier. For example, in 1850 the average of the menarche (first menstruation) in Norwegian girls was 17 years of age; in 1950 it was 13. The average age of puberty had dropped four years in one century. In the United States the average age of the menarche dropped from 14.2 in 1900 to 12.9 in 1950. More recent figures indicate the average has now dropped closer to 12.4 years of age. Thus, a portion of the trend toward younger dating and sexual awareness is a result of this physiological mechanism. I suppose we could slow it down by taking poorer care of our children—but I doubt that idea will gain much sympathy.

Adolescence Is an Age of Inferiority

Your preadolescent youngster should be told the meaning of inferiority and warned about its impact. He or she should understand that perceived inadequacy is an unnecessary cross that most adolescents carry, even though they seem to be happy and contented. There is no greater service a parent can perform for a preteenager than to defuse the self-worth crisis before it arrives, so that it appears universal and temporary. "Nearly every teenager feels inadequate," the child should be told, "and you may go through this stage, too. If you do, remember that it is part of the process of growing up and doesn't really have much to do with genuine self-worth."

There is no greater service that a parent can perform for a preteenager than to defuse the self-worth crisis before it arrives, so that it appears universal and temporary.

I believe that society's false values should be discussed openly. If your youngster knows where the pain is likely to occur, he or she can build defenses against it. By contrast, the lonely adolescent who is never informed about inferiority gets hit from behind by an awful gloom that springs without warning from the darkness. It need not be so.

Adolescence Is an Age of Conformity

The pressure to follow the whims of the group (called the "herd instinct") is never so great as during the adolescent years. This drive may be all-consuming to a teenager when any deviation from the "in" behavior is a serious breach of etiquette. And there is tyranny in this pressure. If the group says one brand of sports shoes is out, woe be to the boy who doesn't get the message soon enough. If a girl talks or walks funny, she may be the object of scorn. Therefore, each teenager knows that safety from ridicule can only be found by remaining precisely on the chalk line of prevailing opinion. The youngster whose emotional needs and self-doubt are great dare not risk defying the will of the majority on even the most trivial matter.

The influence of peer pressure is best illustrated by a study of teenagers conducted by Ruth W. Berenda. She and her associates brought ten adolescents into a room and told them they were going to study their perception (how well they could see). To test this ability, they planned to hold up cards on which three lines were drawn. The lines were marked A, B, and C and were of three different lengths, as illustrated below. Line A was the longest on some cards, while lines B or C were longer on others. The students were to raise their hands when the pointer was directed at the longest line. The instructions were simple and were repeated: "Raise your hand when we point to the longest line."

What one student didn't know, however, was that the other nine had been brought in early and told to vote for the second longest line. The purpose was to test the effect of group pressure on the lonely individual.

When the nine teenagers voted for the wrong line, the lonely individual would typically glance around, frown in confusion, and slip his or her hand up with the group. The instructions were repeated, and the next card was raised. Time after time, the self-conscious student would sit there saying a short line is longer than a long line, simply because he or she lacked the courage to challenge the group. This remarkable conformity occurred in about 75 percent of the cases and was true of small children and high school students. Berenda concluded that "Some people would rather be president than right," which is certainly an accurate assessment.

A _____	
B _____	
C ___	

The same desire to look and think like other teenagers causes problems for those who can't conform. I knew a blind, fifteen-year-old girl who refused to admit she had a handicap. She would not accept the help of a special teacher provided by the school, and her parents could not even get her to use a white cane. To thump along the corridor marked her as different from her peers, and she couldn't tolerate the distinction. I watched one day as she walked to her next class with her head erect, as though she knew where she was going. Before I could stop her, she walked straight into a post. Even this experience was insufficient to make her use a device that other teenagers did not need.

Similarly, I worked with the parents of a second-grade boy with a hearing problem. He simply would not let them put a hearing aid in his ear. He would rather be deaf than different. Truly, conformity is a powerful drive in children of all ages. Even adults succumb to the pressures of what's "in" or "out" according to the media. Long hair, short hair, long skirts, short skirts, wide ties, narrow ties, sweat suits, suspenders—we go to great expense to avoid the embarrassment of being "unfashionable."

Adolescent peer-group pressure accounts for some of the strain between generations and reduced parental influence during this time. I have seen parents feel "hurt" because their developing teenager suddenly seemed embarrassed to be with them. "I went to the door of death to bring this kid into the world," a mother may say, "and now he grows up to be ashamed to even be seen in my presence." She should understand that teenagers are engulfed by a tremendous desire to be adults, and they resent anything that implies they are still children. When they are seen with "Mommy and Daddy" on a Friday night, for example, their humiliation is almost unbearable. They are not really ashamed of their parents; they are embarrassed by the adult-baby role that was more appropriate in prior years. Parents would do well to accept this healthy aspect of growing up without becoming defensive about it.

My own mother understood this process well, and she made use of it for her own purposes. When I was in the ninth grade, I suddenly discovered that it was much more fun to fool around in school than to work and cooperate. So for that one year I played and laughed and irritated my teachers. But I didn't fool my mother. I don't know how she got her information, but she knew that I had gone giddy. One day she sat me down and said, "I know what you're doing in school. I know you're playing and causing trouble. However, I have decided not to do anything about it. I'm not going to punish you or threaten you or even call the principal. But if the school ever calls me, I am going to go with you the very next day. I'll follow you to all your classes and sit in the seat beside you. I will hold your hand and tag around you throughout the day. Just remember my promise."

Believe me, friends and neighbors, that straightened me out quick! It would have been social suicide for my mama to follow me down the halls of Adolescent High School. I'm sure my teachers wondered why there was such a remarkable improvement in my behavior during the last half of my fourteenth year.

It is important for your preteenager to know about group pressure before it reaches its peak. Someday he may be sitting in a car with four friends who decide to shoot some heroin. Your preparation is no guarantee that he will have the courage to stand alone in that crucial moment, but his knowledge of peer influence could provide the independence to do what is right. I would, therefore, recommend reading and discussing this section with your ten- or eleven-year-old.

Adolescence Is an Age of Confusion

A small child is told what to think. Those formative years are subject to the attitudes, biases, and beliefs of parents, which is right and proper. In this way parents fulfill their God-given responsibility to guide and train. However, there must come a moment when all these concepts and ideas are examined by the individual and either adopted as true or rejected as false. If that personal evaluation never comes, the adolescent fails to span the gap between "What I've been told" versus "What I believe." This is one of the most important bridges leading from childhood to adulthood.

It is common, then, for a teenager to question the veracity of the indoctrination received. There comes a moment to ask, "Is there really a God? Does He know me? Do I believe in the values my parents have taught? Do I want what they want for my life? Have they misled me in any way? Does my experience contradict what I've been taught?" For a period of years, beginning during adolescence and continuing into the twenties, this intensive self-examination is conducted.

Your preadolescent should be forewarned about the distress that may be experienced during this period of questioning. It is truly an age of confusion, for nothing can be considered absolute or certain. Parents should brace themselves for this experience. It is difficult to sit on the sidelines and watch your child scrutinize the values to which your life has been dedicated. The process will be much less painful for everyone, however, if both generations realize that the soul-searching is a normal, necessary part of growing up.

Adolescence Is an Age of Identity Formation

Much has been written about the "search for identity," but I doubt if your ten-year-old has read much of that literature. Consequently, you will need to talk about what it means to know yourself. The child with a good sense of identity is acquainted with personal goals, strengths, weaknesses, desires, hopes, and dreams. He could sit down and write a paper entitled, "Who am I?" without bogging down in the first paragraph. A child who has been given a meaningful self-awareness by parents and teachers knows where he's going and how he expects to get there. This is a fortunate individual in this day of gray, indistinct self-awareness.

I would like to describe a less fortunate person, whom I have known professionally. You know him too, for he lives in every neighborhood, attends every school, and is a member of every church. Perhaps 5 million carbon copies are walking the streets of America, with slight variations. This teenager, whom I'll call Jon, was neither the first nor the last child born into his family, making him merely one of a group (or a crowd) at home. His parents were extremely busy during his early childhood, and their effort went into the necessities of living. They read to Jon very rarely and never viewed him with any distinct pride. They just let him grow up on his own. His physical features are not grotesque, but he is certainly no Prince Charming either. In school, Jon immediately had trouble learning to read. He couldn't explain why, but the message didn't get through. He didn't actually fail, but his academic work was hardly worth remembering. His teachers thought of him not as an individual but as a member of that 30 or 40 percent of uninspired students who have to work harder to achieve the same result. In fact, it was easy to forget that Jon was even there.

As Jon came through elementary and junior high school he never excelled in anything. He did not star in Little League. He never learned to make model airplanes. He rarely had more than one or two casual friends at a time. He didn't win awards. He was not chosen class president. He did not learn skills from watching his father. He never did anything for his parents to brag to the neighbors about. His childhood was invested primarily in television and comic books and tree-climbing.

Then little Jon suddenly became Big Jon during his fifteenth year. Pimples and blackheads besieged his face. His nose developed a slight hook to the left. The boys considered him a bore, and the girls could look right through him without noticing that he was there at all. He went out for basketball in the fall, but the coach was busy working with the talented boys. He quit the next day, "because it wasn't interesting." His posture was poor, and his manners were appalling. And he had never given one serious thought to the future beyond high school.

Jon and all those he symbolizes reaches his sixteenth year totally lacking in personal identity, except for a nebulous self-disgust. He does not know who he is, what he wants, or where he is going. At this point his vulnerability to social suggestion reaches a peak. Any group that offers a sense of identity may be adopted *in toto*. They may be skinheads, a street gang, or dabblers in the occult. They offer Jon everything he lacks. In return for his allegiance, they give him a bevy of friends, a sense of power, an accepted "in-group" language, perhaps a uniform, and certainly a set of values and attitudes. In one stroke, they can take a meaningless, bland teenager and instill in him a definite, prescribed (though antisocial) identity.

It is your job as a parent to provide your child with a healthy identity during the formative years in the home. How is this accomplished? By helping discern strengths and interests. By teaching a solid foundation of beliefs and appropriate behaviors. Perhaps most important, by giving compensating skills (see pp. 107–114, 224–28). If you don't do this job, somebody else will.

Adolescence Is an Age of Fluctuating Emotions and Personality Changes

The adolescent experience is typically characterized by a cycle of emotional "highs" and "lows." These mood fluctuations can be disconcerting to other family members, who must learn to live with alternating depression, elation, and everything in between. Perhaps most distressing is the inconstancy of maturity during this time. One day a fifteen-year-old may think and act like a grown-up; the next day the child takes over again.

If each family member is taught to recognize the fluctuating personality pattern as "normal," they might find it easier to live with the emotional, excitable, impressionable, erratic, idealistic, flighty, daydreaming romanticist known as an adolescent.

Adolescence Is an Age of Sexual Fascination and Fear

Perhaps the most important conversation to be held in preparation for adolescence will deal with the sexual awakening your child is about to experience. If you have been doing your job through the years, this final presentation represents a review of matters the two of you have discussed many times before. It is appropriately called a "final" presentation because it may be your last open interchange on this delicate subject. Whereas most topics can be approached directly with a ten-year-old, there probably will be more resentment and embarrassment in having the same conversation about three years later. After a child undergoes the emotional, hormonal, and anatomical changes of puberty, your job as primary sex educator will probably be a thing of the past. In a sense, then, the prepubertal discussion about sex is similar to a coach giving advice to players immediately prior to the big game. He says, "Remember what I've taught you, and don't forget the rules of the game. Let's go over the fundamentals one more time." The coach knows that after the game begins, there will be little opportunity for further instruction.

This vital discussion about sex is much too important to attempt without planning and forethought. In fact, all through the formative years, spontaneous opportunities appear for which your preparation must already be invested. It may be helpful to review the checklist of ten subjects cited below in preparation for the discussions I've recommended. You should have a good notion of what you will say about each of these topics:

1. The role of intercourse in marriage
2. Male and female anatomy and physiology
3. Pregnancy and the birth process
4. Nocturnal emission ("wet dreams")
5. Masturbation
6. Guilt and sexual fantasy
7. Menstruation
8. Morality and responsibility in sex
9. HIV and other sexually transmitted diseases
10. Secondary sex characteristics brought about by glandular changes: pubic hair; general sexual development; increased interest in sex; and similar topics

Since few parents can claim to be experts in sex education, I would strongly recommend a solid preparation through one or two books that specialize in this area. Several excellent books and videos are usually on the market for teens and their parents. They can be reviewed or ordered at a library or large bookstore. A pastor or counselor likely can suggest appropriate sex education materials. A good church library should have at least one title on adolescent sexuality.[1]

There often is a close link between irresponsible sexual activity and low self-esteem, which underscores the urgency of teaching proper attitudes and behavior with regard to the opposite sex. It has been shown repeatedly that adolescents with the greatest sense of inferiority are often the most vulnerable to sexual experimentation and exploitation. Sociologists John Gabnon and William Simon found that the least popular students are most likely to be sexually promiscuous. Having never felt social acceptance, they leap at the first person who offers affection in exchange for intimate privileges. However, the same inadequate teenagers—especially girls—soon find that their sexual availability brings only a momentary sort of attention, followed by more unhappiness. Dr. Emery Breitner agrees. He studied adult "swingers" who engage in wife swapping and other extramarital forms of sexual intercourse. Most of his subjects openly admitted that they were looking for love, companionship, approval, and acceptance. He concluded that promiscuous people want to be loved all the time and try to achieve this through sex.

In her book *Your Child's Self-Esteem*, Dorothy Corkille Briggs stated it succinctly:

> The evidence suggests that the best insurance against indiscriminate sexual behavior when the herd instinct runs high in adolescence—when sexual urges are intense—is a high degree of personal worth. A sense of personal value insulates a youngster from selling himself short and lessens interest in irresponsible sexual behavior.[2]

Obviously, we as parents need to work on both sides of the equation: Reduce the inferiority and teach healthy sexual attitudes.

Adolescence Is an Age of Increasing Independence

It will be helpful to discuss with your child the "breakaway" process that is about to occur. I would suggest a description similar to this: "Paul, you were born into our family as a completely helpless, dependent infant. Throughout your childhood, your mother and I have guided you and taught you what we believe is right. But we won't always have a parent-child relationship as we do now. Within about ten years, you will probably be living away from home, earning your own money, and making your own decisions. You will become an adult and will probably have a family of your own to care for. Sometimes this process of growing up and becoming responsible for your own life puts a great strain on a family. Many times a child wants to grow up too fast for his own good—making decisions he isn't ready for—and parents have to hold back and slow him down. Other teenagers want to go on living at home, taking food and clothing and shelter from their parents, but they don't want to be told what to do anymore. These tensions put a crunch on the whole family, sometimes making loved ones angry at each other.

"The reason I'm telling you this is because I want you to understand what is happening if this kind of feeling comes between us. It won't last forever. In fact, it can be avoided if we keep talking to each other and trying to understand the other side. There are, then, several things I want you to remember: First, I am going to give you a little more freedom each year, as I think you are ready for it. There will be certain things that you will have to accept as long as you live at home, and you will not always like the rules that are established here. However, your mother and I will gradually allow you to make more of your own decisions as you grow older.

"Second, as your freedom increases, so will your level of responsibility. I'll expect you to carry more and more of the family workload, and you'll earn a greater percentage of your own spending money. This responsibility will help prepare you for successful adult living.

"Third, if you ever feel we are being unfair with you during the teenage years, you are free to come to us and express your feelings. You can say what you really think, and I'll consider your viewpoint. However, I will never honor a temper tantrum. If you slam doors and pout and scream, as many teenagers do when they get upset, you'll find my ears completely closed.

"Fourth, above all, remember that you are tremendously loved, and everything that we do will be motivated by that affection. Even if we get upset with each other in the years to come, that deep love will always be there. I look forward to these last years you'll have at home. Before we know it, you'll be gone, and we'll only have memories of these happy days together. Let's make the most of them as a family."

Such a conversation should serve to pacify at least part of the rebellion that often accompanies the adolescent experience. Adolescence can be a more tranquil experience for the family that prepares properly for its arrival. To ignore its approaching onset, however, is like riding up a roller coaster for the first time, not knowing what awaits at the top of the incline. The trip down can be harrowing for everyone on board. There is a better way.

Questions and Answers

We have a fourteen-year-old daughter who is going through the worst of what you've described. She feels ugly and tremendously inferior. She hates herself and everyone else. Her personality is sour, and she is depressed most of the time. It is obviously too late to "prepare her" for adolescence; she is drowning in it right now! What can we possibly do to help her?

Yours is the toughest job in parenthood. The danger is that your child may seek to deal with her feelings in ways that will bring her greater trouble, such as through drugs, an early marriage, dropping out of school, running away, or identifying with an antisocial group of some type. Your love and subtle guidance are more important to her right now than at any other time in her life, though magic solutions are rather scarce.

First, when the despair is as intense as you describe, I strongly recommend that you seek to place your child in a group therapy class. Teenagers have such remarkable influence on each other that they can help pull themselves out of an emotional ditch. Furthermore, it will be refreshing for your daughter to hear, firsthand, that other teenagers have exactly the same feelings and fears that she has experienced. Finally, there is great emotional release to be found in being able to talk about her frustrations and anxieties within the accepting atmosphere of the group. Your high school counseling office should be able to help you locate an appropriate group in your area.

Second, I would suggest saying this to your troubled daughter: "Sometime when you are all alone, it would be a good idea to sit down and list all the things you don't like about yourself. Be sure you have a big stack of blank paper, because you're probably going to need it. No one will ever see this paper but you, unless you reveal it, so you can be completely honest. Write down all the things that bother you, and then place check marks by the matters that worry you most.

"When this has been done, come back through the list and think about each item. Give your greatest creative thought to what might be done to change the things you don't like. If you wish, you might share the paper with our pastor or your school counselor or someone else in whom you have confidence. That person can help you map out a plan for improvement. You'll feel better for having faced your problems, and you might even find genuine solutions to some of the troublesome matters.

"Now we come to an important step. The key to mental health is being able to accept what you cannot change. After you've done what you can to deal with your problems, I feel you should take the paper on which the most painful items are written and burn it in a private ceremony before God. Commit your life to Him once more—strengths and weaknesses, good points and bad—asking Him to take what you have and bless it. After all, He created the entire universe from nothing, and He can make something beautiful out of your life.

"The words of Bill Gaither's song express this thought perfectly:

> Something beautiful, something good,
> All my confusion, He understood.
> All I had to offer Him was brokenness and strife,
> But He made something beautiful of my life."[3]

Our teenage daughter has become extremely modest in recent months, demanding that even her sisters leave her room when she's dressing. I think this is silly; don't you?

No, I would suggest that you honor her requests for privacy. Her sensitivity is probably caused by an awareness that her body is changing, and she is embarrassed by recent developments (or the lack of them). This is likely to be a temporary phase, and you should not oppose her in it.

Must I act like a teenager myself in dress, language, tastes, and manner in order to show my adolescent that I understand him?

Emphatically not! There is something disgusting about a thirty-five-year-old "adolescent has-been." It wasn't necessary for you to crawl on the floor and throw temper tantrums in order to understand your two-year-old; likewise, you can reveal an empathy and acceptance of the teen years without becoming an anachronistic teenybopper yourself. In fact, the very reason for your adolescent's unique manner and style is to display an identity separate from yours. You'll turn him off quickly by invading this identity, leading him to conclude, "Mom tries so hard, but I wish she'd grow up." Besides, he will still need an authority figure on occasion, and you've got the job!

There seems to be so much gender confusion in our society. Pop stars blend male and female qualities. It is considered bigoted not to accept homosexual and transsexual lifestyles. How can I keep my kids from being adversely affected by all this?

You probably experienced an early stage of this social movement when you were a teenager. There has been a steady progression toward total gender confusion over the last three decades, and it is now well ingrained in Western society. Although fashions have come and gone, the trend has been toward an erasing of the distinctions of sexual identity in hair length, manner, interests, and occupations. Such similarity between men and women causes great confusion in the minds of children with regard to their own sex-role identity. They have fewer distinct models to imitate and are left to grope for the appropriate behavior and attitudes.

There can be little doubt that this blurring of roles is contributing to the homosexual epidemic, and it is a frightening trend. Dr. Charles Winick, professor of anthropology at Clay University of New York, studied two thousand cultures and found fifty-five characterized by sexual ambiguity. Not one has survived. Dr. Winick feels the future of Western culture is at stake in this issue, and I am inclined to agree.

In regard to our children, I firmly believe in the value of teaching traditional male and female roles during the early years. To remove this prescribed behavior for a child is to further damage his or her sense of identity, which needs all the help it can get. Masculine and feminine roles are taught through clothing, close identification with the parent of the same sex, and to some degree, the kind of work required and the selection of toys provided. I am not suggesting that we panic if a girl doesn't enjoy playing with dolls or a son prefers art over baseball. It certainly is acceptable for a boy to wash the dishes and a girl to clean the garage. But we should gently nudge our children in the direction of appropriate sexual roles.

My answer to your question will meet violent opposition among many who want to see the differences between men and women disappear. I strongly disagree with this movement. According to my understanding of the divine plan, as explicitly stated in the Bible, the two sexes are ordained for specific masculine and feminine roles that cannot be ignored without painful consequences. Men and women are *equal,* but not *equivalent.* They have equal human worth but are designed for distinctly different responsibilities. It is my prayer that North America will not abandon that inspired purpose at this delicate point in its history.

What causes homosexuality? Can homosexuality ever result from a single, traumatic experience? What can parents do to prevent this tendency in their children?

Despite all the shouting to the contrary, no credible scientific research has substantiated the claim that homosexuality is genetic or innate. The causes of homosexuality, as they are known, are too complex to treat in the context of this book. As a generalization, it is believed that homosexuality can result from a home life that usually involved confusion in sexual identity. Again, conditions vary tremendously, and the active recruitment to the lifestyle that is going on in some quarters has muddied the waters. I think we can still say that the most common home environment of a future male homosexual is a home where the mother is dominating, overprotective, and possessive, while the father rejects and ridicules the child. The opposite situation occurs too, where the mother rejects her son because he is a male. Generally, the same kinds of role confusion in the home contribute to female homosexual tendencies. In some sense, the girl feels rejection because of her gender and comes to believe only a male identity carries worth.

Homosexuality (or at least serious gender confusion) can also result from a rape or other traumatic experience, but there is no evidence that it happens often. I worked with one homosexual teenager whose drunken father forced him to have sexual intercourse with his mother following a New

Year's Eve party. His disgust for sex with women was easy to trace. Most cases are less obvious.

The best prevention of gender confusion remains a strong home life. Homosexuality is much less likely to occur in the context of a loving home where parents are reasonably well adjusted sexually themselves. I don't think it is necessary to react with paranoia even in this aberrant culture. If parents provide a healthy, stable home life and do not interfere with the child's appropriate sex role, homosexuality is less likely to occur.

Has good sex education reduced the incidence of promiscuity and sexual irresponsibility among teenagers?

Of course not. Teenagers are sexually better informed today than at any time in human history, but the traditional boy-girl game seems to be as popular as ever. Two assumptions are being made in education—both badly mistaken. One is that sex education is necessary because kids inevitably have sexual intercourse, and we have to protect them from HIV and other diseases through education and easily available condoms. Studies show that this "safe-sex" ideology not only fails to reduce the incidence of premarital sex; it actually increases it. This program has been supported by nearly three billion dollars of federal support here in the United States, and the result has been disastrous. We had two sexually transmitted diseases at epidemic proportions at the start. There are now more than twenty that plague us. Twenty percent of all Americans now have incurable sexually transmitted viruses! One of the reasons is because condoms break frequently and are too porous to offer real protection against the virus that causes AIDS. The other faulty assumption is that physiologic information will inhibit sexual activity. This is about as foolish as thinking an overweight glutton can be helped by understanding the biologic process of eating.

I am in favor of age-appropriate, values-based, parent-involved sex education—but I have no illusions about its power to instill responsibility in adolescents. Morality, if it is valued, must be approached directly, rather than through the back doors of anatomy and physiology. Of much greater potency is a lifelong demonstration of morality in all its forms by parents whose very lives reveal their fidelity and commitment to one another.

Part 3

Practicing the Strategies

8

A Message for Discouraged Adults

The primary focus of this book is the prevention of inferiority in small children at home and school, but we should pause to comment briefly on similar problems in adults. A poor self-concept is extremely common among adults, and I think it is particularly prevalent among women in North American societies, the geographical area with which I am most familiar. If you are reading from a South American, European, African, or Asian context, there may be nuances of difference, but I think the same principles generally apply. Certainly problems with confidence are universal. Many of the women I have counseled have expressed feelings of low self-esteem. To verify this observation of widespread personal dissatisfaction, I created a questionnaire some years ago entitled "Sources of Depression among Women." Ten items were listed, as illustrated below:

Sources of Depression among Women

Please rank the following sources of depression according to their applicability in your life. Do not sign your name.

	Irritant	Your Rank
1.	Absence of *romantic* love in my marriage	
2.	In-law conflict	
3.	Low self-esteem	
4.	Problems with the children	
5.	Financial difficulties	
6.	Loneliness, isolation, and boredom	
7.	Sexual problems in marriage	
8.	Menstrual and psychological problems	
9.	Fatigue and time pressure	
10.	Aging	

The questionnaire was administered to two groups of white, middle-class wives and mothers, totaling about seventy-five individuals. Their average age was about thirty years. They were asked to mark their answers in complete privacy. When the results were calculated, the first group had clearly indicated "low self-esteem" as the most common source of depression, and the other group marked it a close second.[1] These results were even more surprising when it is considered that the participants were primarily healthy, happily married, and attractive. Most of them confessed a Christian faith. No wonder feminism has found such fertile ground on which to build its political and social agenda. It promises to confront just this issue, though I don't think it has made more than a superficial dent in this fact of Western culture: Feelings of inferiority and inadequacy are still constant companions of many, perhaps most, American women today.

Feelings of inferiority and inadequacy are constant companions of many, perhaps most, American women today.

Crises of confidence appear to be less common in men than in women, but the problem is certainly not exclusive to females. It has surfaced in places where it would be least expected. I once lectured before faculty and students at a seminary on the subject of inferiority, since they would deal with many such problems in their congregations. I relayed the story of "Danny," a distressed high school student whose grief over his inadequacy became intolerable and eventually turned to anger. After I spoke, I received the following anonymous letter:

Dear Dr. Dobson—

I am one of the "Dannys" you spoke of in chapel today. Believe me, for I have experienced this for as long as I can remember. It is a miserable way to live.

Yes, I'm a student at the seminary, but that doesn't make the problem any less acute. Through the years, particularly the last five, I have periodically gained a revived hope that somehow (?) this problem can be overcome—go away or something. Then to my great disappointment, I find it is still very much a part of me. That's when I lose hope of ever conquering it. I want to be a minister of the gospel and feel that this is God's will. At the same time I am aware of the paralyzing effect this deep problem has upon me. I want so badly to be adequate so that I could better serve God and others.

I wish I could talk with you, even for a short time. However, I realize your busy schedule. At any rate, thank you for coming to the seminary.

Sincerely,
A troubled seminarian

Since this broken young man had not identified himself publicly, I read and discussed his letter with the student body the following morning. Many of the three hundred seminarians seemed moved by his words; for some, it undoubtedly reflected their own predicament as well. Following my lecture that morning, the "troubled seminarian" introduced himself to me. He stood with tears streaming down his cheeks as he spoke of the great sense of inadequacy he had experienced since early childhood. Later, an administrator of the seminary told me that this young man was the last member of the student body he would have expected to feel this way. As I have observed so many times, this sense of inferiority is the best-kept secret of the year. It is harbored deep inside, where it can gnaw on the soul.

Sitting in the audience that day was another student with the same kind of problems. However, he did not write a letter. He never identified himself in any way. But three weeks after I left, he hanged himself in the basement of his apartment building. One of the four men with whom he lived called long distance to inform me of the tragedy. He stated, deeply shaken, that the dead student's roommates were so unaware of his problems that he was not missed for five days!

Not only do laypeople fail to understand each other; it has discouraged me to see how often my professional colleagues (psychiatrists, psychologists, and counselors) have overlooked inferiority as a most obvious root for emotional distress. Lack of self-esteem produces more symptoms of psychiatric disorders than any other factor yet identified.

Many times in my work as a practicing psychologist, I spoke with people who deeply needed respect and acceptance. They needed human affection and kindness as well as emotional support and suggestions for change. Yet, if such a needy patient had gone to Sigmund Freud in his day, the immortal grandfather of psychoanalysis would have sat back in detached professionalism, analyzing the patient's transference and sexual repression. If the patient had sought treatment from Arthur Janov, the innovator of primal therapy, he would have been encouraged to roll on the floor and scream like a baby. In the transactional therapy or "encounter group" movement of the 1960s and 1970s, the person would have been required to assault, and be assaulted by, other members of the group. Believe it or not, early psychiatric conferences actually considered the wisdom of female patients having sexual intercourse with their male therapists! Fortunately professional groups came to their senses and developed strong prohibitions against such "therapy" and other unethical practices. Whenever even the most intellectual professionals abandon an ethical base, they cease to make sense, regardless of their degrees and licenses. No wonder psychiatry has been called "the study of the id by the odd." (No disrespect is intended to those who are more conventional in their approaches.)

The most successful approach to therapy for a broken patient, I firmly believe, is to convey in attitude, encouragement, and words the following message: "Life has been tough, and you've had your share of suffering. To this point, you've faced your problems without much human support, and there have been times when your despair has been overwhelming. Let me now share that burden. From this moment forward, I am interested in you as a person; you deserve and shall have my respect. As best as possible, I want you to quit worrying about your troubles. Instead, confide them to me. Our concentration will be on the present and the future, and together we will seek appropriate solutions."

Suddenly, the beleaguered patient no longer feels alone—the most depressing of human experiences. "Someone cares! Someone understands! Someone assures me with professional confidence that I will survive. I'm not going to drown in this sea of despondency. I have been thrown a life preserver by a friend who promises not to abandon me in the storm." This is real therapy, and it exemplifies the essence of the Christian commandment that we "bear one another's burdens" (Galatians 6:2 RSV).

This same Christian principle offers the most promising solution to your inferiority and inadequacy. A person's own needs and problems seem less threatening when one is busy helping someone else handle theirs. It is difficult to wallow in your own troubles when you are actively shouldering another person's load and seeking solutions to that individual's problems. For each discouraged reader who feels unloved and shortchanged by life, I would recommend a conscious practice of giving to others. Visit the sick. Bake something for neighbors. Use your car for those without transportation. Most important, learn to be a good listener. The world is filled with lonely, disheartened people like yourself, and you are in an excellent position to empathize with them. And while you're doing it, I guarantee that your own sense of uselessness will begin to fade.

If you have struggled with inferiority throughout your life, isn't it about time you made friends with yourself? Aren't there enough headaches in life without beating your skull against that old brick wall of inadequacy, year after year? If I were to draw a caricature that would symbolize the millions of adults with low self-esteem, I would depict a bowed, weary traveler. Over this vagabond's shoulder I would place the end of a mile-long chain, to which is attached tons of scrap iron, old tires, and garbage of all types. Every piece of junk is inscribed with the details of some humiliation—a failure, an embarrassment—a rejection from the past. By letting go of the chain, the traveler could be free of the heavy load that immobilizes and exhausts. But somehow the conviction persists that this weight must be dragged throughout life. As in the case of the troubled seminarian, the weight becomes paralyzing. So the dejected person plods on, digging a furrow in the good earth behind.

You can free yourself from the crisis of confidence if you will but turn it loose. Your feelings are based on a distortion of reality seen through childish eyes.

You can free yourself from the crisis of confidence if you will but turn it loose. Your feelings are based on a distortion of reality seen through childish eyes. The standards by which you have assessed yourself are themselves changing and fickle. During the 1920s, women were seeking doctors' help to reduce the size of their breasts. Now many thousands are worried sick about the effects of silicone implants they had stuffed inside them to improve the original equipment.

Modern women are ashamed to admit that they carry an extra ten pounds of weight, yet Rembrandt celebrated the plump, rotund body. False values! Personal worth is not dependent on the opinions of others or the temporal fluctuating values they represent. The sooner you can accept the transcending worth of your humanness, the sooner you can come to terms with yourself. I must agree with the writer who said: "While in the race to save our face, why not conquer inner space?" It's not a bad idea.

Questions and Answers

I am depressed much of the time and worry about whether or not my children will be affected by my moods. Are children typically sensitive to parental discouragement and depression?

According to Dr. Norman S. Brandes, a child psychiatrist, children are very sensitive to depression in the adults around them. They often become depressed themselves, even though adults think they've hidden their despair. Furthermore, you are watched carefully by your children, who are "learning" how you deal with frustration. You are effectively teaching them, through your own depression, to react similarly in the future.

If your depression is chronic, as you indicate, I would suggest that you seek professional advice. Begin with your physician, who may recognize a physical cause for your constant discouragement. If not, he or she may refer you for psychological assistance. This does not mean you are mentally ill or neurotic. It may indicate nothing more than that you need to examine the things that are bothering you with the help of a competent counselor.

When the women you surveyed indicated that "low self-esteem" was their most common source of depression, did physical attractiveness play a role in their feelings? Don't people get over that sensitivity in adulthood?

Many factors were involved in the poor self-concept of the women surveyed. Many of them reported a lack of romantic affection and appreciation from their husbands, which made them feel unneeded and unloved. Others felt isolated and unfulfilled in their roles as wives and mothers. Women today are told they must be professionals to find value, yet being a wife and mother is, I believe, one of the most important jobs in the world. The stability of a nation actually depends on how well women handle this family responsibility. Nevertheless, after being told repeatedly that child rearing is somehow unworthy of their time, those cast in this mold often feel trapped and unnecessary.

Beyond these reasons, physical attractiveness did have a dominant role to play in the inadequacy indicated on the questionnaire. The necessity for beauty does not end in adolescence. It continues to determine human worth to some degree until late in life. I counseled a young woman who had been a beautiful airline stewardess a few years earlier. She was happily married to a man who was proud of her beauty. Then a most unfortunate thing happened: An automobile accident scarred her face and twisted her body. Her back was broken, and she was destined to walk with a cane for the rest of her life. Since she was no longer attractive to her husband, he quickly lost interest in her sexually. Their divorce followed shortly. As a cripple she could no longer serve as a stewardess, of course, and she found it difficult to obtain a job of any type. In this instance, a girl with high personal worth plunged to a position of little social status in one brief moment. Her true value as a human being should not have been affected by her accident, but it certainly was.

If you doubt the influence of physical attractiveness in your own value system, give yourself the supreme test: Go into an exclusive clothing store, where all the salespeople are beautifully tailored and combed. Walk up to a four-way mirror and examine yourself from all angles. Scrutinize the back of your head, your profile, and your rear end. If you're "normal," this experience will destroy you for at least three days.

While there are many causes for low self-esteem among women, that old nemesis, "the uglies," which every woman experiences at least occasionally, keeps doing its dirty work throughout our society. It may not be the only source of depression, but it remains a major one.

9

Why We Do What We Do

We must turn now, in the concluding pages of this discussion, to the meaning of behavior itself. Have you ever wondered how two children raised in the same home can be so unique and individualistic? How can one child be reverently quiet and withdrawn, while another, produced and raised by the same parents, is noisy and self-assertive? Extending the questions further, what determines the various personality patterns of human beings? Why is one person kind and gentle while another is irritable and hateful? Or in the present context, what are the ingredients from which such lifelong personality characteristics are constructed in a young child?

Longitudinal investigations conducted at the University of Minnesota have attempted to answer those questions by focusing on the fascinating topic of identical twins raised apart. More than 100 pairs have been identified to date, many not knowing the other existed until recently. Since the individuals had the same genetic endowment, any differences evident in adulthood were assumed to have resulted from environmental influences. The surprising finding is that more than half, and perhaps as much as 70 percent, of the basic temperament is attributed to hereditary factors. Your child is the way he or she is because of the characteristics with which he or she was born.

But what about the other contributors to personality? Though they are less influential, environmental factors and family relationships do play a significant role in developing the person your son or daughter will become. It is with regard to this "learned" behavior that your contribution as a mother or father will be made. In order to fulfill your parenting responsibilities properly, you must develop the skill to get behind the eyes of the child, seeing what he sees, feeling what he feels, hoping what he hopes. It is this awareness of his world that permits a parent (or teacher or grandparent) to hold the child when he is threatened, to love him when he is lonely, to teach him when he is inquisitive, or to discipline him when he knows he is wrong. The success of the parent-child relationship depends on this perceptive skill. How often do teenagers complain, "My parents don't understand me!" They are pronouncing judgment on their parents' inability to "mind read" as I've described.

But how can this ability be attained? It is acquired by developing an understanding of the meaning of behavior, which begins with the issue we have been studying—that is, self-confidence and its antecedents. It is the heavyweight of human behavior. Feeling unloved, unworthy, and foolish is one of the most distressing experiences in living. That mental state, which I have called a "crisis of confidence," gnaws on the soul by day and invades the dreams by night. So painful is its impact that our emotional apparatus is designed specifically to protect us from its oppression. In short, a sizable proportion of all human activity is devoted to the task of shielding us from the inner pain of low self-esteem. I believe this to be one of the most dominant forces in life, even exceeding the power of sex in its influence. Therefore, if we are to understand the meaning of behavior in our boys and girls, husband or wife, friends and neighbors—and even our enemies—then we must begin by investigating the ways human beings typically cope with self-doubts and personal inadequacies.

The remainder of this chapter is devoted to the six most common ways children (and adults) deal with inferiority. Most children adopt one or more of these avenues of defense. Each parent is encouraged to look within the following pages for the footprints of his own child, and while doing so, he might even find the sand-filled remnants of his own tracks.

Pattern 1: "I'll Withdraw"

One of the most common ways of dealing with inadequacy and inferiority is to surrender, completely and totally. The individual who chooses this approach has concluded in his own mind that he *is* inferior. He measures his worth according to the attributes we have discussed (and others), making this reluctant admission: "Yes, it's true! I am a failure, just as I feared. Even now people are laughing at me. Where can I hide?"

Having accepted personal unworthiness—the first mistake—the individual is forced to guard his wounded ego from

213

further damage. Thus, "caution" becomes the watchword. The person withdraws into a shell of silence and loneliness, choosing to take no chances or assume unnecessary emotional risks. This person would never initiate a conversation, speak in a group, enter a contest, ask for a date, run for election, or even defend his honor when it is trampled. From the early years on, he copes with inferiority by projecting a defensive meekness, having learned that the best way to save face is to button his lip. As comedian Jackie Vernon once said, "The meek shall inherit the earth, because they'll be too timid to refuse it."

In most school classrooms one can find one or more children who have admitted defeat to themselves. In the elementary grades they sit year after year in silence with eyes cast downward. Their peers know them as "shy" or "quiet" but seldom understand their true feelings. The withdrawing child is usually misjudged in two major ways: (1) Quiet, reserved, and unresponsive, he is frequently assumed to be stuck-up and snobbish. The child who is most overwhelmed by feelings of personal inferiority is blamed for thinking too highly of himself. How little we understand each other! (2) Because the withdrawing individual seldom speaks, it is assumed that he isn't thinking. Quite the opposite, this child's mind whirls with thoughts and feelings like everyone else's. But this person has learned early that the safest defense is to keep the mouth shut. This strategy often backfires for a boy, who becomes the unprotected target of the local bully.

I believe we have much greater reason to be concerned about the withdrawing child, from a psychological point of view, than the more aggressive troublemaker. Children at both extremes often need adult intervention, but the surrenderer is much less likely to get it. He doesn't bug anybody.

He cooperates with the teacher and tries to avoid conflict with peers. But this quiet manner is dangerously misleading. Adults may fail to notice that a destructive self-image is rapidly solidifying and will never be pliable again. Considering all the alternative ways to cope with feelings of inferiority, withdrawal is probably the least effective and most painful. It is, in reality, no defense at all.

The introspective adults who choose this approach are more at risk for hypertension, migraine headaches, acute colitis, and other stress-related illnesses. Their caution prevents them from releasing the emotional tension trapped within, often resulting in a physical blowout somewhere inside. As housewives they pull within the walls of their homes, biting their nails, peeking out at the world passing by, and often weeping in loneliness. They live with depression, and too frequently their only ally is a bottle of booze, leading to secret alcoholism. A man with the same response may become a henpecked Milquetoast. Since he lacks the ego strength to lead the family, he must be content to follow in silence. All in all, extreme withdrawing is not a very successful approach to problems of inferiority.

Considering all the alternative ways to cope with feelings of inferiority, withdrawal is probably the least effective and most painful. It is, in reality, no defense at all.

Pattern 2: "I'll Fight"

The *identical* feelings motivating one child to withdraw from society urge a more aggressive boy or girl to fight in response.

Instead of surrendering to inferiority, like the withdrawing child, the fighter is angry, carries a chip on the shoulder, and dares anyone to knock it off. He looks for any excuse to lash out, and his temper can be triggered by the most insignificant provocation. If he is tough enough to back up the threats, this kid becomes the terror of the playground. Later he may develop into a mean, temperamental malcontent, always looking for a hassle with somebody—anybody. My deepest sympathy is with the person who is married to a confirmed fighter.

Although inferiority is always distressing, the fighter is less vulnerable to its impact than a withdrawing child. The fighter has a defense, even if it is an antisocial one. The realization of this creates the climate for a dramatic personality reversal during the early teen years. Not infrequently, a quiet, timid child will creep into adolescence as a cautious surrenderer. Having avoided conflict all through life, this child has suffered accordingly. Then during the natural antagonism of adolescence, he learns almost by accident that it hurts less to fight than to withdraw. Suddenly, this shy, meek youngster becomes hostile and aggressive. Parents shake their heads in disbelief as their cooperative teenager declares total war on everyone in sight.

When the intensity of inferiority is greatest, the shift from withdrawing to fighting may involve violence and viciousness. Remember the example of Lee Harvey Oswald's life. He attempted to cope with his problems in several ways, but he was blocked at every turn. Running away to Russia (withdrawal) did not help, nor was his predicament eased by submission to his wife (surrender). He was unsuccessful in all his less aggressive attempts at coping. Finally, as often happens, his grief turned to anger. A sudden outburst of aggressive behavior is likely to occur any time a more passive approach has consistently failed to ease the severe pain of inferiority.

The murderer of Robert Kennedy had a remarkably similar childhood in emotional tone. Sirhan Sirhan was "unstable and unhappy" throughout childhood.[1] When his family came to America, he was bothered by his strangeness as a foreigner in the eyes of his classmates. Sirhan's father, Bishara, beat his children with sticks and fists and once held a hot iron to Sirhan's heel. Like Oswald, Sirhan was small in stature, and his method of dealing with inferiority was to withdraw and surrender. He was polite and quiet, concentrated on his studies, and kept out of trouble.

After high school graduation, young Sirhan began a desperate search for adequacy that was no more successful than the quest of Oswald. Because of his slight build and short stature, becoming a successful jockey offered the brightest hope for achieving self-respect, and he invested every ounce of energy in that dream. When he applied for a job at Santa Anita Race Track, officials saw that he lacked the reflexes and experience to handle the temperamental animals. Instead, he was given a job as a "hot walker" and exercise boy, the least respectable job on the track. A "hot walker" leads the horses around the track after they have been running. Even more humiliating, Sirhan frequently fell off his mount, earning him the title of "real-estate buyer" in the jargon of the horsemen. Finally, he was severely injured and taken to a nearby hospital. His humiliation was complete, and he raged at everyone who tried to treat him. Sirhan gave up horses that day; he hadn't even come close to reaching his most cherished dream.

Shortly thereafter he suffered the crowning blow. Sirhan identified himself completely with the Arab cause in the Six-

Day War against Israel. The crushing Arab defeat became his personal loss, agitating him beyond containment. By now the quiet young man who kept out of trouble had become a fighter. Both Kennedy assassins, Oswald and Sirhan, followed the same well-trod pathway:

1. They experienced deep-seated feelings of inferiority.
2. They sought to cope by withdrawal and surrender.
3. Their vain attempts to achieve adequacy were miserable failures.
4. They exploded in violence.

This pattern fits Karl Menninger's description of a typical assassin.[2] Dr. Menninger described "an anonymous, faceless, embittered man who feels self-important and ambitious. He also feels unloved, lonely and alienated. He wants desperately to be somebody but never makes it." These two extreme cases from American history illustrate the dramatic shift from a passive, coping behavior pattern to violence.

The movement from withdrawal to aggression can be seen in other, less deadly instances throughout society. In my opinion, this principle fuels the tremendous hostility in some radical feminists. As a result of societal forces unleashed in worker-short North America during World War II, the importance of being an at-home wife and mother was unnecessarily, even foolishly, devalued. Women who didn't earn a regular paycheck were taught to think: "I'm just a housewife." The burning message of inferiority and even the disrespect of husbands was preached by the media; yet the responsibilities of children and the home made it impossible for millions of women to escape. Suddenly the sense of unworthiness initiated an emotion-charged reversal from acceptance to aggression. It is most unfortunate that wives and mothers were not given the status and respect their position deserves. We have reaped the harvest of broken homes and a weakened nuclear family.

Fighting is an important way of dealing with inferiority, and it accounts for a certain proportion of the violence in our time. It produces much of the antagonism of adolescence, and it is likely to appear whenever less aggressive personality patterns fail to reduce the pain of feeling inferior.

Pattern 3: "I'll Be a Clown"

Another common way to deal with inferiority is to laugh it off. By making an enormous joke out of everything, the clown conceals the self-doubt that churns inside. A great many well-known comedians have turned this pattern into a life career. Rodney Dangerfield epitomizes self-deprecating humor. Interviewed in the mid-1990s about his long career, he was candid about the life-long fears of failure and depression behind the words "I get no respect." The humor in a long-running television comedy, *Roseanne*, was built in part around the weight problems of the female lead. Joan Rivers has joked incessantly about her ugliness as a girl. Phyllis Diller, the frazzle-haired comedienne, was, by her own account, a shy, inadequate, withdrawing youth. Constantly aware of her unattractiveness, she discovered a less painful—and more lucrative—way of coping: through self-effacing laughter. Interestingly, Diller remained very conscious of her appearance throughout her career, having cosmetic surgery when she had "begun to look pretty horrible. Not funny-horrible—just bad," as she explained.

Being a clown is a particularly useful approach for the individual with a very obvious facial flaw. Barbra Streisand has frequently made fun of her nose. But the king of the nose humorists was Jimmy Durante. How would you deal with a Durante nose if it were stuck on the edge of your face? Everywhere you went, people would look at it and laugh. All through childhood you would be hounded about that "pound of flesh" out front. What could you do? Stay furious at the world? Beat up anyone who snickered? Your best bet would be to learn to laugh.

Jonathan Winters's parents were divorced when he was seven, and he used to cry when alone because other children said he had no father. Winters now recognizes the wisdom of Thackeray's observation that "Humor is the mistress of tears."

Teachers are well acquainted with the clowns in the classroom. These skilled disrupters are usually (but not necessarily) boys. They often have reading or other academic problems, may be small in stature, and may do anything for a laugh (eat worms, risk expulsion from school, hang by one toe from a tree). Their parents are usually unappreciative of the humor and may never recognize that the clown, the fighter, and the surrenderer have one important thing in common—feelings of inferiority.

Pattern 4: "I'll Deny Reality"

I worked with the teacher of Jeff, a seven-year-old who wore heavy leather gloves to school every day. He was rarely seen without his gloves, even on the warmest days. His teacher insisted he remove the gloves in the classroom, because he could scarcely hold a pencil with his thickly padded fingers. But the moment Jeff went to recess or lunch, the gloves reappeared. Jeff's teacher could not understand the motive for this behavior. All through the school year Jeff had not wavered in his desire to wear hot, cumbersome gloves. In describing the problem the teacher casually alluded to the fact that Jeff was the only black child in a classroom filled with white children. His feelings suddenly seemed obvious. Wanting to be like everyone else, when wearing a long-sleeved shirt or coat, the only black skin Jeff could see was on his hands. By wearing gloves, he hid the feature that marked him as different. He was, in effect, denying reality. He wanted to conform so badly that he denied the reality of his God-given difference.

This approach is one of the favorite coping behaviors in North American society. It is primarily responsible for the enormous problem of drugs and alcohol. For example, there are somewhere between ten million and thirteen million alcoholics in the U.S. Another eight million are classified as "problem drinkers." About one of four U.S. citizens has a close family member who is a confirmed alcoholic. What better example of emotional escape can there be than living in a drunken stupor most of the time? Undoubtedly, the need for temporary escape plays a key role in the drug-abuse phenomenon that has swept through every age group and socioeconomic sector of society. Adolescents and young adults particularly have fallen prey to drug addictions from crack to prescription medicines. Massive self-doubt simply cannot be ignored. It must be handled in some manner. My work with lifelong addicts in the Federal Narcotics Symposium in Los Angeles confirmed my suspicion of the part played by inferiority in drug dependence.

Another convenient way to deny reality is through psychotic experience. This is not to oversimplify an exceedingly complex illness for which biochemical and other organic factors may be at work. I am convinced, however, that psychosis is, in many individuals, an attempt to pull down a mental shade and withdraw into a personal dream world. Problems do not have to be faced if one refuses to acknowledge that they exist. This experience is the most unfortunate of the alternatives to which individuals can turn.

Pattern 5: "I'll Conform"

One of the great myths in the United States is that we are a nation of rugged individualists. We like to think of ourselves as Abraham Lincoln, Patrick Henry, and Martin Luther King Jr., standing tall and courageous in the face of social pressure. We are fooling ourselves; in truth we are a nation of social cowards. A major portion of our energy is expended in trying to be like everyone else, cringing in fear at true individuality. Dean Martin once said, "Show me a man who doesn't know the meaning of the word *fear*, and I'll show you a dummy who gets beat up a lot!" In our case, however, we are not afraid of being beat up. It is ridicule and rejection that motivate our concern.

We are a nation of social cowards. A major portion of our energy is expended in trying to be like everyone else, cringing in fear at true individuality.

Conformity, then, presents itself as the fifth personality pattern in response to inferiority. Those who adopt it may be social doormats, afraid to express their own opinions. They seem to be liked by everyone, regardless of the expense to their own convictions and beliefs. For adolescents, whom I've already described, the urge to conform dictates most activity for a period of ten or more years. Accordingly, adolescent behavior is the most contagious phenomenon shared from one human being to another. I once watched a teen choir sing "The Battle Hymn of the Republic." The singers were tense under the hot lights, and, as sometimes happens in a live choral performance, one singer near the front row fainted and crumpled to the floor at a high point in the emotional presentation. The director went on with the performance, but now the suggestion of fainting had been planted in fifty-two impressionable heads. Boom! A second singer went down. Boom! Boom! Two more hit the deck. As the mania spread like wildfire, five more vocalists blanched, buckled, and disappeared from the back row. By the time the director reached the last "Glory, Glory Hallelujah!" twenty members of the choir were out cold on the floor. That is conformity at its best.

Conformity also combines with denial of reality to inspire the drug abuse problem—especially among the young. For this reason, the best education programs in the schools will not solve the problem of teen addiction. Most teens today know the consequences of drug usage, probably better than do their parents. The most successful antidrug programs have been those that targeted and sought to marshal peer pressure. One of the first efforts to do this was the "Just say no" campaign. Its critics called the program naïve in proposing such a simple solution. But in a number of student populations it began to make nonuse of drugs the standard of conformity. Peer accountability groups in some schools have taken this a step further.

If one wants to see a classic example of how conformity has changed sides in the adult population, look at the anti-smoking movement. It is definitely not acceptable to smoke, and I suspect the reasons have a lot less to do with health concerns than with peer pressure. To the extent that it has become just as disgraceful to use cocaine or marijuana in some groups, drug use has declined. In large segments of young society, however, the epidemic will continue unabated until someone finds a way to turn the tide on fashion. It won't stop a minute sooner.

Conformity plays a key role in our social life. It offers a readily available response to inadequacy and low self-esteem.

Pattern 6: "I'll Compensate"

I have presented five common personality patterns that often develop to cope with feelings of inferiority. The selection of a particular pattern may not be totally a matter of personal choice. It has always surprised me to observe how rigidly society dictates which of the five approaches an individual is expected to pursue. "Everyone knows," for example, that the fat person is supposed to be a jolly clown. It would seem strange to see an obese person fight or withdraw, because we've come to expect smiles on the faces of our overweight friends. On the other hand, a redhead is told of his or her "hot temper" from early in life and is expected to be a fighter. A girl with a weak chin and soft voice is molded into the withdrawing pattern, whether she likes it or not. A teenager is required to conform, fight, and perhaps deny reality. In fact, adolescents can play all five roles in confusing array because their personalities are in a state of reevaluation and change.

This dramatic social force stamps its indelible image on our psyche. Surprisingly, we do what we're told.

I agree with the wisdom of the old aphorism:

> We are not what *we* think we are.
> We are not even what *others* think we are.
> We are what *we think* others think we are.

There is great truth in this statement. Each of us evaluates what we believe other people are thinking about us, and then we often play that prescribed role. This explains why we wear a very different "face" among different groups. A doctor may be an unsmiling professional with patients, reserved and wise. They "see" their doctor in that mold, and the doctor fulfills their expectations. That evening, however, the doctor is reunited with former college friends who remember the postadolescent screwball. So now the clown emerges. The patient would be amazed and would not recognize this persona. Similarly, most of us *are* what we think others think we are. This makes inferiority more difficult to treat. We not only must change a person's self-concept but also the individual's concept of what everyone else thinks.

But however we follow our perceptions and arrange our personality accordingly, the five personality patterns just described are all more or less maladaptive. They offer momentary methods of coping with inferiority, but the self-doubt lingers. The better alternative is compensation. The unconscious reasoning for compensation goes like this: I refuse to drown in a sea of inferiority. I can achieve adequacy through success if I work hard at it. Therefore, I will pour all my energy into basketball (or painting, or sewing, or politics, or graduate school, or gardening, or motherhood, or salesmanship, or Wall Street—or for a child, elementary school, or piano playing, or computers, or football).

This kind of compensation provides the emotional energy for virtually every kind of successful human behavior, as described earlier. Victor and Mildred Goertzel investigated the home backgrounds of four hundred successful people. The persons selected were recognizably brilliant or outstanding in their respective fields, among them Churchill, Gandhi, Franklin Roosevelt, Schweitzer, Einstein, and Freud. Their "Cradles of Eminence" study found:

1. Three-fourths of the children [were] troubled—by poverty; by a broken home; by rejecting, over-possessive, estranged, or dominating parents; by financial ups and downs; by physical handicaps; or by parental dissatisfaction over the children's school failures or vocational choices.

2. Seventy-four of eighty-five writers of fiction or drama and sixteen of twenty poets [came] from homes where, as children, they saw tense psychological dramas played out by their parents.

3. Handicaps such as blindness; deafness; being crippled, sickly, homely, undersized, or overweight; or having a speech defect [occurred] in the childhoods of over one-fourth of the sample.[3]

It seems apparent that the need to compensate for disadvantages was a major factor in these leaders' struggles for personal achievement. It may even have been *the* determining factor.

Perhaps millions of "inadequate" persons have used compensation to achieve esteem and confidence. Note the story of one of the twentieth century's most influential women, Eleanor Roosevelt.

- Orphaned at ten, her childhood was filled with anguish.
- She was very homely and never felt she really belonged to anybody.
- She was described as a humorless introvert, a young woman unbelievably shy, unable to overcome her personal insecurity and convinced of her own inadequacy.

Mrs. Roosevelt did rise above her emotional shackles. As Victor Wilson said, "from some inner wellspring, Mrs. Roosevelt summoned a tough, unyielding courage, tempered by remarkable self-control and self-discipline."[4] That "inner wellspring" can be called by another appropriate name: compensation.

Obviously, one's *attitude* toward a handicap determines its impact. It has become popular to accept the role of "victim" of whatever adverse circumstances. "Victimized minority" status has been applied to excuse all sorts of irresponsible (and sometimes vile) behavior. For example, poverty *causes* crime; broken homes *produce* juvenile delinquents; a sick society *imposes* drug addiction on its youth. This fallacious reasoning removes responsibility from the shoulders of the individual. The excuse is hollow. We must each decide what we will do with inner inferiority or outer hardship.

Admittedly, it requires courage to triumph over unfavorable odds. Compensation takes guts, for some more than others. The easier path is to wallow in self-pity, to freak out on drugs, to hate the world, to run, to withdraw, to compromise. Regardless of the ultimate course of action, however, the choice is ours alone, and no one can remove it from us. Hardship does not *determine* behavior, but it clearly influences it.

Parents can open the door to responsible "choices" by giving their children the means by which to compensate, beginning during the middle childhood years.

As noted earlier, parents can open the door to responsible "choices" by giving their children the means by which to compensate, beginning during the middle childhood years. If parents do not accomplish that vital task, they increase the probability that their children will adopt one of the less successful patterns of behavior. Of the six alternatives, compensation is by far the best for your child.

Questions and Answers

Can you give some other examples of angry, hostile behavior as a response to inferiority?

Both socially and individually, people respond in anger when they are put in an inferior position for a prolonged time. I have mentioned the anger behind the feminist movement. Various civil rights and liberation movements have been fueled by this anger, based on past perceptions of inferiority. Blacks, Hispanics, and Native Americans have all cried out in rage as they sought to redress earlier wrongs and demand reform. One reason, perhaps, behind the implacable hatred of the West by some Islamic factions is a feeling that Westerners have looked down on their Arab heritage. Certainly this is one factor at work in terrorism, both in the Middle East and against the government in Northern Ireland. We see it in the gay movement, Vietnam veterans groups, organizations of the disabled, and some of the reactionary paramilitary organizations. Whenever people perceive that they are treated as second-class citizens, anger is a common reaction.

History is full of examples. Adolf Hitler told the defeated German people that their loss in World War I was the fault of their leaders and, of course, the Jews; they were, Hitler told them, superior human beings. He capitalized on their wounded pride as a defeated, humiliated people. The Arab armies suffered a humiliating defeat at the hands of Israel in 1967. After the start of the 1973 war against Israel, one Arab journalist was quoted as remarking: "It doesn't matter if the Israelis eventually counterattack and drive us back. What matters is that the world no longer will laugh at us."[5]

Study has strongly shown that feelings of inferiority provide a major force behind the rage of rapists. They seldom seek sexual gratification as an end. Having been unsuccessful with girls through adolescence and young adulthood, they desire to humiliate, demonstrating their sexual superiority by disgracing and exploiting women.

In the late 1990s we have seen examples of the most horrendous violence in schools. A young boy under the influence of friends in a Satanist cult kills two and injures several others with a gun. Another shooter who had trouble fitting in at school fires indiscriminately into a prayer group circle.

Some years ago the National School Safety Center at Pepperdine University estimated that 3 million crimes occur on school grounds each year—from vandalism to rape and murder.[6] As we discussed before, some of this antisocial behavior can be attributed to the frustration of inferiority. Many adolescents let their reactions to mistreatment at home spill out in the classroom. School itself makes many feel ignorant and worthless. In urban schools much of this crime is gang related, and gang violence usually has a self-image component. "As a consequence of indifference and abuse," comments *Time* magazine, "children are left emotionally crippled, self-centered, angry and alienated." Sacramento psychologist Shawn Johnston adds, "These children are dead inside. For them to feel alive and important, they engage in terrible types of sadistic activity."[7]

The examples are legion. That is why I contend that social chaos in all its forms is linked to inadequacy and inferiority. There are numerous other causes, of course, but none so powerful.

You said a person acts according to the way he thinks he is seen. Can parents use this principle to train their children?

Certainly. If you let a child know you think he is lazy, sloppy, untruthful, unpleasant, and thoughtless, he'll probably prove you are right. Obviously, it is better to make him stretch to reach a positive image than stoop to match one at ground level.

My son is only three, and he's still extremely shy. He won't let anyone hold him but his own family, and he can't even look a stranger in the eye. How can I pull him out?

At his age, shyness is nothing to worry about. He is retreating to the safety of the familiar because he is threatened by the new. That's a reasonable maneuver. It would be a mistake to tear him loose from the security of your arms too quickly, although you should begin to move in that direction. If his shyness and bashfulness continue unchecked through the next year, I would recommend that you utilize the time-honored approach of preschool to help with the task. It would be wise to introduce him gradually to a good preschool program, accomplished in four distinct steps:

1. Talk about the exciting things he will soon do in preschool. Try to whet his appetite during the two weeks prior to entry.
2. Take him to visit the teacher at least twice, perhaps on consecutive days, when no other children are involved. Tip off the teacher to the name of his dog or cat and other familiar topics they can discuss.
3. Let him observe the other children in play from the sidelines with you standing nearby. No interaction with other children is required on this day.
4. The fourth step brings "plunge-in" day—even if he yells bloody murder when you leave. His peers will do the rest.

Shyness in a three-year-old is not unusual and does not warrant concern. If it does become necessary to pry him loose in the years that follow, it will better be accomplished by nudging rather than ripping his moorings.

Specifically, would you rather your own child "withdraw" or "fight"?

That is like asking if I would rather my child have the mumps or the measles. Both are rather like diseases, and I prefer neither. Extreme withdrawal and extreme aggression are both signs of emotional pressure. If forced to choose between these two patterns of behavior, however, I would take the fighter. His discomfort is likely to be more manageable.

10

The Only True Values

Finally, we return to the point at which we began—with the question of human worth. Having rejected physical attractiveness, intelligence, and materialism as determiners of value, we must now decide what will take their places. Have you consciously examined the principles you are teaching to your children? Are you following a well-conceived game plan on their behalf, instilling healthy attitudes and concepts? That instructional responsibility is much too important to handle in a haphazard manner.

Without question, the most valuable contribution parents can make to children is to instill in them a genuine faith in Jesus Christ. What greater source of confidence can there be than knowing that the Creator of the universe is acquainted with us personally; that He values us more than the possessions of the entire world; that He understands our fears and anxieties and reaches out to us in immeasurable love when no one else cares; that He turns our liabilities into assets and our emptiness into fullness; that He sent His only Son to die for us and has promised us life eternal, where handicaps and inadequacies will be eliminated and pain, suffering, and tears will be no more than dim memories.

What a beautiful philosophy with which to "clothe" a child. What a wonderful message of hope and encouragement for the depressed teenager who feels crushed by life's circumstances. This is self-worth at its richest, not dependent on the whims of birth or social judgment or the cult of the superchild, but on divine decree. If this be "the opiate of the people," as Karl Marx sneered, then I have staked my entire life on the validity of its promise.

Not only is Jesus Christ the source of all meaning in life, but He is the only one who can free us from the tyranny of the self. Christian principles place the spotlight on others rather than on ourselves, while granting human worth on a completely different scale of values than does society. The Master never told us that the beautiful people have an inside track. He never granted special favors to intellectuals. He is not partial to the wealthy. He is unimpressed by blue-blood family heritage. In fact, He expressed disdain for such values in Luke 16:15: "For that which is highly esteemed among men is abomination in the sight of God" (KJV). In other words, God actually hates the things that we value most highly, because He sees the folly of our worshiping that which can be kept for such a brief time.

But what *does* God value? We cannot substitute His system for ours unless we know what He has personally ordained. Fortunately, the Bible provides the key to His value system for humankind. It seems to be composed of seven all-important principles:

1. devotion to God;
2. love for others;
3. respect for authority;
4. obedience to divine commandments;
5. self-discipline and self-control;
6. humbleness of spirit; and
7. repentance and forgiveness through a personal relationship with Jesus Christ.

These seven concepts are from the hand of the Creator, and they are absolutely valid and relevant for today. When applied to life, they encourage a child to *seek* out opportunities rather than *hide* in lonely isolation. They lead not to despair, as do humanistic values, but to emotional and physical health. Isn't this what Isaiah meant when he wrote, "And all thy children shall be taught of the LORD; and great shall be the peace of thy children" (Isaiah 54:13 KJV)?

The healthy self-concept Christ taught involves neither haughtiness nor self-loathing. It is one of humble reverence for God and every member of the human family. We are to see our fellow human beings as neither better nor worse than ourselves. Rather, we are to love them as ourselves, and that prescription puts the entire matter of self-worth into its proper perspective.

Notes

Chapter 1: The Epidemic of Inferiority

1. *Focus on the Family* radio program, airdate May 4, 1984.

Chapter 2: Beauty

1. Deborah A. Byrnes, "The Physically Unattractive Child," *Childhood Education* (December 1987), 80–85.

2. Amy Russell, "When You're Born a 2.5 Instead of a 10," *Glamour* (October 1987).

3. Ellen Berscheid and Elaine Walster, "Beauty and the Best," *Psychology Today* (March 1972), 44–45. The article cites research by Karen Dion.

4. John Camp, "The Importance of Being Pretty," *Health* (June 1989), 82.

5. Berscheid and Walster, op. cit.

6. Deborah A. Byrnes, "The Physically Unattractive Child," *Childhood Education* (December 1987), 80–85. Condensed in *Education Digest* (May 1988), 32.

7. George Orwell, *Animal Farm* (New York: Penguin, 1951), 114.

Chapter 3: Intelligence

1. James Dobson, *Dare to Discipline* (Wheaton: Tyndale House, 1973), 133–35 of the 1970 printing. Used by permission.

Chapter 5: Defuse the Values Bomb

1. These estimates were reported by the NEA for 1993. To add another disturbing perspective to that picture, *Time* (13 January 1992, p. 18) reported a Centers for Disease Control statistic that one in five high school students was packing a gun, knife, or club on any given school day. We should note that since these fearsome reports in the early 1990s, many schools have taken strong initiatives to reduce the number of weapons on campus.

2. Philip Elmer-DeWitt, "The Amazing Video Game Boom," in *Time* (27 September 1993), 68.

3. Bruce Handy, "Why Johnny Can't Surf" and "America Online's Little Problem," in *Time* (15 December 1997), 75–76.

4. Lewis J. Lord and Miriam Horn, "The Brain Battle," *U.S. News and World Report* (19 January 1987), 60.

5. See the comments of Neil Postman and other analysts in "Is TV Ruining Our Children?" *Time* (15 October 1990) and "Are Music and Movies Killing America's Soul?" *Time* (12 June 1995).

6. Interview with Susan Littwin, *TV Guide* (1 July 1989), 20–22.

7. Ibid.

8. Marie Winn, *Unplugging the Plug-in Drug* (New York: Viking Penguin, 1987), xiv–xv.

9. Rick Barry, *Confessions of a Basketball Gypsy*.

10. Kathryn Simmons, "Adolescent Suicide: Second Leading Death Cause," *Journal of the American Medical Association* (26 June 1987), 3329.

11. Simmons, op. cit., citing the theory of Paul C. Holinger and Daniel Offer.

Chapter 6: Parent Positively

1. Dobson, *Dare to Discipline* (Wheaton: Tyndale, 1973).

2. Mike Michaelson, ed., *Growing Pains* (American Academy of Pediatrics, 1969).

3. *Glamour* (October 1987), 58–59.

4. Marcy O'Koone, "Are You Smarter Than You Think? Probably!", *Good Housekeeping* (August 1988), 190.

5. Neala S. Schwartzberg, *Parents* (May 1987), 118.

6. Ibid.

7. Sheila Tobias, "Tracked to Fail," *Psychology Today* (September 1989), 55.

8. Ibid., 57.

9. Marguerite Beecher and Willard Beecher, *Parents on the Run* (Santa Monica, Calif.: DeVorss, 1983).

Chapter 7: Help the Teenager Succeed

1. I am aware that many parents do not feel capable of conducting a talk about sexuality or some of the other topics in this preadolescent training section. In an attempt to assist this task, I recorded a series of cassette tapes for young people called *Preparing for Adolescence* (original publisher, Ventura, Calif.: Vision House, 1978). Accompanying the tape is a workbook and two tapes just for parents. These materials are designed to stimulate further discussion and interaction. They are available through bookstores and the retail division of Focus on the Family.

2. Dorothy Corkille Briggs, *Your Child's Self-Esteem: The Key to His Life* (New York: Doubleday, 1970).

3. Bill Gaither, lyricist, "Something Beautiful, Something Good," copyright © 1971 by Wm. J. Gaither.

Chapter 8: A Message for Discouraged Adults

1. For other results from this questionnaire, see James Dobson, *What Wives Wish Their Husbands Knew about Women* (Wheaton: Tyndale House, 1975).

Chapter 9: Why We Do What We Do

1. Reported by Paul O'Neil in "Ray, Sirhan—What Possessed Them?" *Life* (21 June 1968), 33.

2. Quoted in Albert Rosenfeld, "The Psychobiology of Violence," in *Life* (21 June 1968).

3. Victor Goertzel and Mildred Goertzel, *Cradles of Eminence* (Boston: Little, Brown, 1978).

4. Newhouse News Service.

5. "The World Will No Longer Laugh," *Time* (22 October 1973), 49.

6. Richard N. Ostling, "Shootouts in the Schools," *Time* (20 November 1989), 116.

7. Anastasia Toufexis, *Time* (12 June 1989), 52–58.